T0369251

# WHISPERING PINES

*Linda Walker*

WestBow
PRESS
A DIVISION OF THOMAS NELSON

WestBow Press books may be ordered through booksellers or by contacting:

WestBow Press
A Division of Thomas Nelson
1663 Liberty Drive
Bloomington, IN 47403
www.westbowpress.com
1-(866) 928-1240

Scripture taken from the New King James Version. Copyright 1979, 1980, 1982 by Thomas Nelson, inc. Used by permission. All rights reserved.

ISBN: 978-1-4908-0313-5 (sc)
ISBN: 978-1-4908-0312-8 (hc)
ISBN: 978-1-4908-0314-2 (e)

Library of Congress Control Number: 2013915691

Printed in the United States of America.

WestBow Press rev. date: 09/06/2013

# WHISPERING PINES

As I was in prayer one morning, I got out my prayer journal and began to write things that were on my heart to the Lord. I remembered hearing a preacher say that if we make and keep appointments for different things, why not make an appointment to spend time with the Lord? He said, "Set aside some time in your life to spend quiet time with the Lord." So I started doing just that.

I began my prayer time with my Bible and journal. I would read the Word, and then I would write my prayers and petitions to him. As I wrote, he spoke to me through my spirit. I began looking forward to my quiet times with the Lord.

At first, I wrote mostly my petitions. But as I continued spending time with him, he communed with me. I felt his presence each time I fellowshipped with him. Thoughts came to my mind that I knew were not my thoughts. The Lord would speak a verse from Scripture, a word of encouragement, or a song, sometimes it would be something for me to pray about, also letting me know how much he loves and cares for me.

We all are searching for the presence of the Lord; being in his presence is so awesome. As I sat quietly in his presence, he revealed to me that he was aware of everything that concerns me, that he was my Father and has great love for me, and that I am never alone.

I pray that this book will bless and encourage you to make that appointment with your heavenly Father. He is waiting to fellowship with you. He has an awesome plan for your life and wants to guide and keep you on the path that he has prepared for you.

He is waiting for you. Join me as we draw near to the Father and hear his heart.

*Make Room for Me*

# 2012

# JANUARY

# January 05

Make room for me.

Father, thank you for speaking to me yesterday about putting on the tallith (prayer shawl) when I pray. Thank you for speaking to me in the evenings through my dreams.

Help my son and daughter-in-law make the right decisions concerning their finances. I ask for your perfect will to be done in their lives and for their children. Bless our children and grandchildren, and keep your hedge of protection around them.

Bless our new business, and bless Fred. Keep him strong and healthy, and keep us balanced. I ask that you also give us time to rest and time to spend together. Thank you for strengthening our marriage and causing it to be as days of heaven upon this earth.

Cause this family, our children and grandchildren, to be close and grow closer and more loving each day. Bless our family, Lord, with your richest blessings and your presence, joy, peace, and love.

I ask that you reveal to me what you want me to do. Let me know each step and your plan for my life. I know that you told me to preach the gospel to the world; show me the next step, and cause us to be in agreement. Thank you for the privilege to tell hurting people that you are the answer to all their problems. Release me now Lord. The business of the secretary. Righteousness exalts a nation. "Kingdom principles." (Magazine article).

"Let not your heart be troubled, neither let it be afraid." John 14:27. Thank you, Lord, for our new home and for pouring your blessings upon us. Thank you for giving me the desires of my heart. In Jesus' name. Amen.

# January 10

Father, thank you for your Word. Help me, Holy Spirit, to enter into this rest. I need to hear from you concerning my children and grandchildren. My desire is for us to be so close. I desire for all yokes to be destroyed in each of our lives so we may love one another and walk together in unity and oneness of heart and purpose. My desire is for our family to also draw closer to you, Lord, and to put you first in our lives and serve you. Guide us in the plan you have for our lives.

I pray to know your perfect will for my husband's and my lives and for us to obey you in everything. Thank you for our freedom from all bondage and for helping us to live in total peace and contentment, as led by your Holy Spirit. Thank you for the success of our new business.

"Humble yourself under the mighty hand of God and He will exalt you in due time." 1Peter5:6. "Peace, be still." Mark 4:39. "Grace, grace, God's grace, grace that is greater than all my sins."(By Julia H. Johnston.) "Hope thou in ME." Psalms 42:11. "Delight yourself in the Lord, and He will give you the desires of your heart." Psalms 37:4. Help is on the way. "My hope is in you, Lord." Psalm 39:7. My help is in you, Lord.

On Christ, the solid Rock, I stand. He fills my every longing and keeps me singing as I go. Oh, the riches of the inheritance of the saints in the light. We owe no man anything but to love him. Love never fails. "Cause me to hear your loving kindness in the morning, for in you I do trust. Cause me to know the way in which I should walk, for I lift up my soul to you" (Psalm 143:8).

# January 12

Father, thank you for healing me and touching me with your presence today.

Thank you for my happiness and for helping me to lose the weight that I needed to lose.

Wonderful Counselor, mighty God, everlasting Father, Prince of Peace, thank you for healing my mom. Give her joy and peace.

# January 16

Father, please touch Kathryn and heal her. Thank you for her healing and for giving Peggy and Rich peace. Thank you for providing Terry with the job that you have for her. Thank you for your provision for all of us and for loving us. I draw near to your heart. Thank you for meeting our every need and for protecting us.

# January 17

Thank you for this day, Father, and for the privilege of being able to keep my granddaughter Lila today. What a joy. Heal her, Lord. Thank you for blessing me with all of my grandchildren. Continue to bring all of them to us. What joy they bring us. We love them so much.

Thank you for blessing us with our marriage, family, home, and businesses. Help me to be a good steward over all that you have given me. Blessings chase the righteous and overtake us. Bless the work of our hands. Forgive all my sins. Wash them away by your blood. Unify this entire family, Lord, and your blessings be upon us forevermore.

I am clothed with glory and honor and long life. You will satisfy me and show me thy salvation. Blessed be my rock. When my enemies rise up against me, you defeat them for thy name's sake. (Harbinger.)I will read this book Lord. My destiny is with you. (Levitical priest).

I love you, I love you, I do, heavenly Father, for all that you do. Worshipping and calling upon your name, heavenly Father. I'm worshipping your name. Worshipping, worshipping with all that I am. Worshipping, worshipping, forever I am. Come and go with me. Come and fly with me to the place you will always be.

My Excellency, my jubilee, I will forever and ever be with thee. Come, my love. Come to the place you will always be with me. I worship the King; I worship the King. My life is with you forever. With you, two kingdoms will be together. With you, my Master, my Savior, my King, I worship you. I worship the King, my Savior, my Lord. Together we'll stand forever. Together we'll stand.

# JANUARY 18

My goal, Lord, is for you to show us how to become debt-free. Thank you for helping us with that. I speak in the confidence that we are already debt-free. Thank you for destroying every yoke of bondage in our lives and in our family members' lives.

Thank you for restoring us all in Jesus' name. Thank you that we all clearly hear from you, draw closer to you, and walk in the Spirit. Give us all unity, peace, and love, Lord. You are my Deliverer, my Help, my Guide, my High Tower. You are the Lord who blesses, restores, and heals. My Master, my King, my Lord.

My all-consuming Fire, Prince of Peace, Lord of Lords, bright Morning Star. Your name is wonderful, Jesus, my Lord. Rock of ages, almighty God is he, strong deliverer and soon-coming King. Bow down before him, love and adore him. His name is wonderful. Jesus, my King, matchless Savior, and Rock of all ages, I run to you just as I am. My Master, my Savior, my Friend. Thank you, Lord, for setting me free.

# JANUARY 19

Father, I pray for my friend. You have called her to be a pastor and have anointed and delivered her. Father, give her peace. Heal her from her brokenness over those who have left, help her to overcome, and set her free from any offenses. Show her that you are for her and with her and that you will build the ministry you have for her. Forgive me for questioning her correction. I release all that to you, Father, and I forgive all!

Thank you for healing and mending our friendship. Bless all the work of her hands. Bless her marriage, family, church home, and all she does for you. May wealth and riches be in her house Thank you for her anointing, gifting, love, and prayers. I ask you to bless her beyond anything she could ask or think. Give her joy, Lord—comfort, peace, and love. May she be led by the guidance and presence of your Holy Spirit every day of her life. Thank you for all that she has done for me, poured into me, and blessed me with for so many years. Thank you for our friendship. In Jesus' name.

Blessings shall surely overtake us. We march to a different beat of the drum. Heal my mom's broken heart.

Minister of the gospel, strong delivery. Every word spoken over me shall come to pass. Wealth and riches shall be in our house. I forgive all.

# JANUARY 24

All is well! Thank you, Father, for speaking to me last night through the prophet, speaking a word to me and telling me what you would have me to do. Thank you, Lord, for all the teaching you've allowed me to be taught and hearing all of the Word that has been spoken to me over the years. I pray that all of the seeds sown into me, my husband, and my children will bring forth a hundredfold harvest.

Remember the saints. Remember the prophets. "Occupy until I come." Luke 19:13. Keep praying and speaking God's Word. Sweet communion, sweet anointing. Watchtower, multiply me exceedingly. Help me with the next step in the completion of the book. Give me favor with the publishing of the book. Help me make the right decisions and make right choices. Lead me every step of the way.

Thank you for my friend Pastor Elizabeth. Bless her for all she has poured into my life, in teaching and ministering and training. "Great peace have those who love thy law, and nothing shall cause them to be offended". Psalm 119:165. "Righteousness exalts a nation." Proverbs 14:34. "Blessings chase the righteous and overtake us." Deuteronomy 28:2. Such peace and undisturbed composure, mighty God. All is well.

Such awesome peace I never knew till I met you.

# January 25

Thank you, Lord, for putting people in my path who will help us with our new home.

Protect our home and marriage and family. Help me to always do what is pleasing in your sight. Thank you for blessing me; help me to be a blessing to others.

I put a shield of protection upon me and my marriage and family.

Thank you for your blessing upon our businesses, more than we could ever ask or think. Your presence is all I want and all I need. "Blessings chase the righteous and overtake us." Deuteronomy 28:2.

Draw my brother to you by your Holy Spirit, Lord. "On the wings of a snow-white dove, he sends his pure, sweet love. Sent from above, on the wings of a dove." {Bob Ferguson}.

My love awaits you.

# January 26

Father, you are my rest. "Come to me, all you who labor and are heavy laden, and I will give you rest. Take my yoke upon you and Learn of me, for my yoke is easy and my burden is light." Matthew 11:28.

I hide myself in you. I find rest for my soul. "Peace I leave with you, my peace I give to you; not as the world gives do I give to you." John 14:27. My peace I give to you. Triumphal entry. Thank you for your direction, Lord. Relieve my soul. The peace of God passes all understanding. Your holy hill.

Forgive me for all my sins. Heal me and I shall be whole   Mercy Mountain Boys.

I am in you, I am in you, I am in you today. I Am in you, Holy Father. Please show me the way. " Give, and it shall be given to you: good measure, pressed down, shaken together, and running over; will be put into your bosom." Luke 6:38. In thee I plead, Heavenly Father; in thee I plead. Praise the Lord, I am whole. No fear ever again in my life.

"To whom much is given, much is required." Luke 12:48.

Flying away with you, ever increasing in my endeavoring to do your will with purpose, power, and might. Waves of glory wash over me. Gentle breezes, candle of the Lord. Fasting.

Valley of triumph, wash away my sin. Inner ear of revelation, wax cold.

Valley of indecision, help is on the way. Watchtower kaleidoscope.

Wonderful Savior, mountain of love.

# JANUARY 27

Father, thank you that all that I do, I do for you. Watch over me and help me and give me favor: favor with the publishing of the book and with the company.

Be with my mom. Heal her and help her to go forward with her life, not look back. Help her overcome her sadness of losing my dad. Put joy in her heart and heal her. Give her purpose to keep living, and give her peace. May she feel your love every day.

"Mercy triumphs over judgment." James 2:13. May you put whom you want in the office of the president, a God-fearing man who will seek you first and submit to your direction.

With God, all things are possible.

Shout to the Lord with a voice of triumph! Shout, for he has given you the city.

*Bashan* means *smooth soil*, the name of a vast highland east of the sea of Chinnereth (Sea of Galilee).

Blessed are you, you sons of David. Great wealth and riches are yours, possessors of heaven and earth. Blessings chase the righteous.

# JANUARY 28

Thank you, Father, for protecting my children and grandchildren today as they go on their trip. Protect my husband as he goes and comes back from his meeting. Thank you for our anniversary too, Lord. Great and marvelous peace do I have.

Thank you, Father. Thank you for setting me free. Such joy, such peace have I.

Blessings chase the righteous and overtake us. Give me direction with the book, Lord. Help me with all the decisions. Give me favor with answering the questions, financing, and selling the book. Millions of copies of my book shall sell, in Jesus' name. "Blessed are the righteous their seed shall be mighty upon this earth. Wealth and riches shall be in their house." Psalms 112:2-3.

Johnnie on the spot   Deep commitment wash over me, wash over me today. Wash over me, wash over me, I pray. Wash over me today. Blessed Redeemer blessed Redeemer, Shirley (Mom). Wash over me, wash over me, wash over me today.

*Linda Walker*

You are the sunshine of my life; you are the apple of my eye. Bright and morning star you are. Amen.

# January 31

Thank you, Father, for another year of health and wealth and happiness and growing closer to you, Lord, each day. Be with my mom today as she has a procedure on her eyes. Guide the doctor's hands and give her peace.

Thank you, Lord, for protecting this family, watching over us, and keeping us safe. "Great peace have those who love your law, and nothing shall cause them to be offended." Psalms 119:165.

Father, cause the people to vote the way you would have them vote. Put the man in office whom you would have be in office, who will stand for what is right and be led to do what you want for this nation.

Thank you for favor, kindness, guidance, and direction. Give me wisdom concerning the book. It is yours. Thank you for giving it all to me. I ask that it bless many, many millions of people. May they draw closer to you and seek you more intimately.

Be with Fred and I as we go on this trip. Thank you for protecting us as we travel on the plane. Surround us and give us favor with all.

# FEBRUARY

# FEBRUARY 01

Father, thank you for your forgiveness and for giving me such joy and peace. Make me a blessing to my husband and family and all around me. Thank you for my children and grandchildren; I love them so. This family flourishes, walking in love and forgiveness.

"Blessings chase the righteous and overtake us." Deuteronomy 28:2. "Righteousness exalts a nation." Proverbs 14:34. "Mercy triumphs over judgment." James 2:13. Washington, DC, one nation under God, with liberty and justice for all. March madness, watchtower. We are to be in prayer for this time and season.

It is your will that I rest in you, in your wondrous abundance of peace and prosperity. The wealth of the wicked is ours now; prosperity belongs to us, and wealth and riches are in our house. Blessed are the righteous. Their seed shall be mighty upon this earth.

"I lift up my eyes to the Lord, where my help comes from. My help comes from the Lord, maker of heaven and earth." Psalms 121:2. "Come, let us reason together." (Levitical priest). Isaiah 1:18.

# FEBRUARY 02

Thank you, Father, for the spiritual revelation of Fred and I being one. I honor him and value him. He is priceless to me. Thank you for giving him to me as my gift. I ask that our love grow stronger and more intimate each day. May our bond of unity be strengthened each day. May our marriage be as heaven upon this earth for us and our family.

Widespread famine. Parenthetical, watchtower, firm foundation.

Bright and morning star you are. Commonwealth of Israel.

# FEBRUARY 03

Thank you, Father, for healing Lila, my granddaughter. Touch her, Lord. Thank you for giving her words of wisdom. May she be every bit whole.

*Washington Post.*

Whitney Pheps. I lift him up to you in prayer today Lord.

# FEBRUARY 04

Thank you for healing us, Lord. Join our family together as one.

"Righteousness exalts a nation." Proverbs 14:34. Revive us again. "A closer walk with thee, precious Jesus, is my plea. A daily walk with thee, O Lord, let it be."{Elijah Cluke}.

A prophecy is coming to pass.

# FEBRUARY 07

"This is my story; this is my song. Praising my savior all the day long. This is my story; this is my song praising my savior all the day long." {Blessed Assurance by Fanny J. Crosby}.

Thank you for blessing us with so much, and for blessing our business and the success of it.

Time spent with you serves much purpose. We are enriched and basking in your love. Worship the King.

Wonderful Savior   March madness.

I am blessing you when I give of food, clothing, shelter, help, or blessing. I am giving to you. Bold petitions.

Blessings chase us and overtake us. In Jesus' name.

Majesty. Life-changing power; effervescent, enchanting, ever-increasing faith.

# FEBRUARY 08

Watchtower, perpetual harvest.

Thank you, Father, for our harvest and all the blessings you have showered upon us. How rich we are. I desire your presence, love, wisdom, and revelation.

O what a wonder you are, matchless Savior, mighty God. Draw near to all.

Merciful Savior, peaceful praise, rest assured   mega fest.

# FEBRUARY 09

Thank you, Father, for healing me, delivering me, and blessing me, my husband, and my family with more than I could ever have imagined. Help me to honor and reverence my husband. I appreciate all that he does for all of us. Bless him, Father, for the godly husband, man, father, and provider he is to me and this family. Thank you with all of my heart for blessing my life with him. Bless him each and every day of his life. Cause him to be full of joy, wisdom, and peace. Make his feet like a hind's feet, running up to the mountaintop to be in your presence every day of his life. Fill him with your pure river of life.

May our children be blessed more and more every day because they worship and love you, Lord. May they and our grandchildren be strong in your might. May they do exploits, miracles, signs, and wonders in the power of your name.

Life is in the blood. Wichita, Kansas.

"Righteousness exalts a nation." Proverbs 14:34.

# FEBRUARY 10

March madness. I believe that you are letting me know that we are to be in prayer at this time for this season.

# FEBRUARY 13

Father, thank you so much for the publisher accepting my book (*My Journey*). You gave it to me and it is yours.

Thank you for giving me favor with it. Help Fred and I make wise decisions concerning it.

I ask that many, many books will sell—that millions will be sold—and many, many people will be helped. May they be delivered and draw closer to you, Lord. Give me favor with all the people that I will be working with at the publishing company. Breathe your blessing upon it. Bless all who read it. May they seek you and draw closer to you. May they hear your voice, come to you, give their lives to you, and be saved.

Wesleyan Methodist—all of those who doubt. Believe. Help me learn from you and trust that you will do it. Valley of decision.

# FEBRUARY 15

Eagleton Press.

Father, lead me my Shepherd. Help me to know all avenues to take for the promotion of this book. You know the right paths for me to take. I trust your care for me. Grant me the best printing for this book. Give me favor with all aspects of it. Help me in the marketing of it.

Blessed prophet, quick and easy, you will give them hope who has no hope. "My yoke is easy and my burden is light. Take my yoke upon you and learn from me." Matthew 11:30. Wesley Methodist. "My people are destroyed for lack of knowledge." Hosea 4:6. Lord, give me your wisdom and knowledge. Cornerstone Baptist Church.

The best is yet to come. Soldiers of the cross. Serendipity. (Finding valuable or pleasant things not looked for.)

# FEBRUARY 16

Thank you, Lord, for your guidance and direction from the Holy Spirit. Sing me a new song.

Matchless Savior. I will use Facebook to market my book. I go forth in the power of your might.

Bask in my love and see yourself as I see you: confident, well-adjusted, and free from man-pleasing. Adjusted and brave, strong and courageous, bold as a lion, a light shining in darkness. Come rain or shine, I am thine.

# FEBRUARY 16

"He who calls you is faithful, who also will do it." 1 Thessalonians 5:24. "Come before His presence with singing and into His courts with praise." Psalms 100:2. "Beloved, I pray that you may prosper in all things and be in health just as your soul prospers". 3 John 1:2. Surely I will be with you.

# FEBRUARY 20

Thank you, Father, for the vision you gave me of Mom the other night. She looked so happy and pleased. I believe you were showing me how happy she is with me and how pleased she is that I wrote the book. Thank you for that vision. How that blessed me and encouraged me!

Thank you for healing me, Lord, and thank you for giving me peace. Thank you for being with Fred and me as we go on our trip. Thank you for giving us safety, going and coming and while we are there.

"May they prosper who love you." Psalms 122:6. Thank you for the anointing that destroys yokes and removes burdens in our lives. Perpetual harvest. Washington, DC.

"The blessings of the Lord, it maketh rich, and he addeth no sorrow with it." Proverbs 10:22. Meet with me.

With all that is within me, I worship you. Richness is of the Lord; wealth is of the Lord.

"Be it unto me according to thy word." Luke 1:38.

# FEBRUARY 21

It is you I want to please.

# FEBRUARY 22

Thank you, Father, that as I go, you go with me. You will protect, guide, comfort, and bless me with your presence and anointing. Speak to me, Lord, and give me your instruction. Help me to obey you in everything you tell me to do.

Protect us as we go to this meeting. May we shine as bright lights representing you, my King.

Thank you for a wonderful day today with Mom and Terry. Thank you that the publisher got back with me today concerning the book, so we can move forward. Thank you for your anointing and blessing upon the book. Thank you for the success of it and for the doors it will open. In Jesus' name.

# FEBRUARY 24

I ask that Fred and I have a very blessed time together in your presence. May we be in total agreement about the publishing of this book. May he support me and encourage me to continue to go forward. May we experience total peace as we fly to this meeting and as we are in Las Vegas. Give us favor with his company. May we have a wonderful, blessed, and prosperous time together in you, Lord.

Protect our children and family. Give them rest and give us rest, Lord. Refresh us in your presence.

May blessings continue to be upon our businesses, our lives, and our ministry.

Weather the storm. Fill this place with your presence. There is no fear in love.

# MARCH

# March 06

Thank you, Father, for the breakthrough. Thank you, Father, for favor with the publishing of the book. Give me favor with each person who touches the book. Thank you for the turnaround in our lives. John Wesley. Thank you for your anointing upon the book, in what I say and where you send me. I come to the river. I thirst and hunger for you, Lord. A vessel filled with the fullness of you, Lord.

Richness of you, Lord; fill us to overflowing . Move in this family. Move blessing and comfort.

Give my sister comfort and direction, healing and provision. Provide the job you have for her. Open the door and provide a new residence for her, Lord. Give her a place she can call her home. Give her peace and happiness. Fill her with your presence. Guide her and help her in every decision she makes. Help her to seek you in all she does. May she feel that she is worthy and loved by you and her family. May she feel your love and care. Deliver her and bring complete joy and fulfillment in her life. Bring that special someone in her life, one she knows loves her completely. May she look to you for direction, to meet her every need and turn everything around in her life.

Blessed be the Lord, who always gives us the victory.

Rags to riches. "Wealth and riches shall be in our house," Psalms 112:3. Riches and honor.

# March 08

I know what you have instructed me to do. I will obey you, and blessings shall be upon me.

Juniper. "Tidings of comfort and joy." {William B. Sandys}. You're the rock on which I stand. Copyright.

Endeavoring to do your will, Lord. Multiplied by hundreds of thousands. Jack of all trades.

I know I hear your voice. I know that you direct me. Speak to me and give me your perfect will for my life, you direct my every step. Shall I write in the quarterly magazine? Will the messages come?

"With God, all things are possible." Matthew 19:26. "For precept must be upon precept, precept upon precept, Line upon line, line upon line, here a little and there a little." Isaiah 28:10.

A little help from my friend, Vital Vision. Purpose-driven life.

# MARCH 11

Thank you for protecting Terry tonight as she travels home. Protect her on the road and in the hotel. Give her peace and sweet sleep. I love you and thank you for restoring this family. I will speak what you say. Abundance of peace, and with a long life I will satisfy them and show them my salvation. March madness

"Great peace has those who love thy law, and nothing shall cause them to stumble (or be offended)." Psalm 119:165.

Great is the peace of my children. From warrior to saint.

You will never leave me and never forsake me. Jack of all trades. I worship you, my King. Mississippi mud pies. Great Jehovah, my soon-coming King. What a wonder you are.

You shine as the morning star; Jesus, what a wonder you are. Emanuel: God with us.

Blessed Redeemer, Living Word. Righteous Father, Master, Savior. Righteous Judge.

# March 13

Dear Jesus,

Thank you for what you have done for us. Thank you for your blood that heals me. Thank you for forgiving me of my sins and for washing me clean. Thank you for your presence in my life. Thank you for leading me and guiding me. Thank you for the Holy Spirit, who helps me, counsels me, teaches me, and brings things to my remembrance. Thank you, Father, for speaking to me. Thank you for your plans for my life and my family's lives. Thank you for giving me such joy, peace, and love.

Blessed assurance: Jesus is mine. I am blessed beyond measure. Make me a blessing today to all.

"Blessings chase the righteous and overtake us." Deuteronomy 28:2. "Goodness and mercy shall follow me all the days of my life." Psalms 23:6. "Be it unto me according to thy word." Luke 1:38. Thank you for the turnaround today.

Restoration today. Ministry, success of this book, and success of our businesses. It is as you say.

Living water, rescue. Dominican Republic. Glory to behold and riches to behold.

# MARCH 20

"By wisdom, a house is built, and by understanding, it is established; by knowledge the rooms are filled with all precious and pleasant riches." Proverbs 24:3-4. "Many are the afflictions of the righteous, but God will deliver us out of them all." Psalms 34:19. March madness.

Riches and honor. May the book minister to and help a lot of people, I pray. May I be more concerned about people's lives being changed and helped than anything else. May everyone who reads the book draw closer to you, Lord, and desire to know you more intimately.

Blessings and honor, riches and honor. All is well.

# MARCH 23

Thank you for love and forgiveness, for direction and counsel. Thank you for bringing me people who guide me and help me make right decisions. Guide Terry by your Holy Spirit and heal her broken heart. Help her also make the decisions that you would have her make.

Thank you for the new books. Thank you for your peace. Total restoration. Peace, joy, love, and forgiveness.

# MARCH 24

I worship you, my King. Multiple blessings. Multiplied by tens of thousands.

Enrich our lives with your presence. Riches and honor and the favor of the Lord.

Blessings and honor. Not one will be missing. "Do unto others what you would have them do unto you." Moral rectitude. Soon-coming King. Wisdom from above. Great peace.

Wisdom, knowledge, revelation, and understanding.

# March 26

Father, thank you for healing my knee. Worship the King. Who am I to come out?

Marvelous Lord, merciful Father, soon-coming King.

Thank you for the success of our businesses. Blessings overtake the righteous.

"Righteousness exalts a nation." Proverbs 14:34. More of your presence Lord.

"And the Lord restored Job's losses when he prayed for his friends. Indeed the Lord gave Job twice as much as he had before" (Job 42:10).

Double.

Thank you for the open door. "In this world, you will have tribulation, but be of good cheer. I have overcome the world."

# MARCH 30

How majestic is your name in all the earth, o Lord. Thank you for restoring, healing, and prospering us all. Thank you for your loving kindness, for your mercy, and for your goodness.

Mercy ministries. "Mercy triumphs over judgment." James 2:13. Wichita, Kansas. Light pierces darkness.

# APRIL

# April 01

Father, thank you for answering my prayers and for total restoration.

I pray and ask you, Lord, for our family to walk in unity and love.

Guide us to make right decisions. Help us to know that we are where we are supposed to be at this time in our lives.

Show us your bright and shining way. Have thine own way, Lord. Everyday miracles, merciful Father. Righteous one, righteous one.

"Blessings chase the righteous and overtake us." Deuteronomy 28:2.

# April 03

Thank you, Father, for all of the songs that you gave to me last night: sweet songs of praise and petition to you. Songs of peace, love, and joy filled my heart. I know how much you love me and want to spend time fellowshipping with me. Thank you for teaching me that when you are finished with something, I should not keep trying to make it live. You are wanting to do a new thing in my life. It is a new day. I need you to direct me every step of the way. Help me to make wise choices that will bring you glory. Direct me, Lord, to the next step, for others.

March madness.

A new day, a new way, a new start.

We live to give and to be a blessing.

(*The Good Life Magazine.*)

"Apple of my eye." Psalms 17:8 Thank you, Father, that Fred and I have gone to the next level.

Up to a higher level with you Lord.

# April 05

Thank you, Lord, for all you have done for all of us. For taking my sins and sicknesses and

diseases and pains and all the evils of this world upon you. I worship you and manifest your presence in my life and my family's lives today.

Bright and shining star is who you are. I worship the King. Unity, love, and harmony. Bright and morning star is who you are. "Mercy triumphs over judgment."

Much corn, much harvest.

# April 09

Shall I speak to our pastor concerning the book *Whispering Pines*?

Thank you for the richness of the Lord.

# April 11

Thank you, Lord, for waking me this morning, and for the dream you gave me, and for letting me know about Mom. When it is time for her to go home to be with you, she will be with you for all eternity. Comfort her and this entire family today. Lord, restore us all.

Thank you, Father, for my family. I forgive all. Bless my children, my grandchildren, my husband, our marriage, our businesses, the books, and all that you have given us to be good stewards over.

Bless the Lord, who always causes me to triumph. Songs of deliverance. Worship the King.

Rhapsody. All your waves wash over me with your love.

# April 13

I pray for my sister Terry today, Lord. Be with her as she faces knee surgery. I ask that you guide the doctor's hands and that she will have a speedy recovery. Give me understanding of the dream that you gave me this morning.

Obedience. Totality.

# April 17

Father, how I thank you for helping me. Thank you for giving me favor yesterday with the book and with the Web site. Thank you for favor with you and man. Wisdom, might, strength, and the fear of the Lord. Glory to your name. I ask that you protect the book and our family. Cause the book to be successful and for people to grow closer to you. May they be blessed with hope and peace. I ask that many, many people will come to you, Lord. I ask that there be no persecution or propaganda. In Jesus' name.

Wealth and riches shall be in our house. Our house is built on the Rock, Jesus Christ.

Riches and honor and the fear of the Lord belong to us.

Pleasant places. Money cometh.

Don't settle for anything less than my best for you. Riches and honor belong to you.

Restoring all!

# APRIL 20

Make my spirit rich. Bless our business today. Much happiness. Unique name. Set my husband free from feeling sad or overwhelmed or lonely. Fill him to overflowing with such joy every day of his life. Wash over us with your love.

Honor me. "Occupy until I come." Luke 19:13. Continue doing business until I come. Uncontrollable love. Wisdom, righteousness, sanctification, and redemption. Unified.

# APRIL 23

"Blessed be the Lord, who always causes us to triumph." 2 Corinthians 2:14.

"Mercy triumphs over judgment." James 2:13.

# APRIL 24

Thank you for bringing me out and birthing the new thing that you are doing in my life. My life is yours. Help me be a blessing to others. Thank you that I cannot go back to where I was, because I am now not that person. Thank you for the new door that you are opening for me. I walk through this open door, full of grace and mercy. Called and chosen by you to be your handmaiden, I am blessed, anointed, highly favored, protected, and loved. The very presence of God goes before me and behind me. Wisdom, righteousness, sanctification, and redemption belong to me. We shine as a bright light in the darkness.

Glory to you, Father.

"Behold, I give you authority to trample on serpents and scorpions and over all the power of the Enemy and nothing shall by any means harm you." Luke 10:19.

# APRIL 25

Father, I have favor with you and man. You have opened the door for me. Help me to recognize what is of you and what is not of you. Guide us in your perfect will and comfort those who mourn in Zion.

Wash over me.

Wash over me.

Wash over me with your love.

Wash over me, wash over me.

Wash over me with your love.

Fulfill all your purpose in me, Lord, and bring it to pass in my life.

Your ways are not my ways, Lord.

Sweet sleep belongs to me.

# April 28

Your presence is my desire. To just sit and fellowship with you, fill my heart and home with your love and presence. Hope for a brighter day. Draw those who don't know you. Draw them to you by your Holy Spirit.

Bless our children and our grandchildren today, Lord. Thank you for the rich blessing they are in my life. How I love them and praise you for blessing us with them.

You have blessed me with such happiness and gladness of heart by giving me my husband and family. What a huge blessing they are in completing my life. Thank you for being so real in my life and giving me peace, joy, love, wholeness, and contentment. This is a priceless gift from you. I praise you for the richness of your love and presence in my life.

# April 30

You are my Ambassador, my soon-coming King. Please give me everything you want me to say in the next message, "the faith factor." All of it is from you, Lord.

Worship the King. I have confident expectation. I can do all things through Christ, who strengthens me.

Behind the veil.

Help me to be that encourager, that exhorter, that comforter who will build up others.

Help me to be a vessel filled with your love and a vessel fit for your honor. You make all things brand new.

Let your request be made known unto God.

"Come unto me, all you who labor and heavy laden, and I will give you rest. Take my yoke upon you and learn from me, for I am gentle and lowly in heart, and you will find rest for your souls. For my yoke is easy and my burden is light." Matthew 11:28-30.

"Cast your bread upon the water." Ecclesiastes 11:1.

# MAY

# May 03

Thank you, Father, for your favor and protection for my family. Draw all of us close to you.

We seek your face. How blessed I was yesterday to see the beautiful cover of the book. How wonderful it truly is. May it bless many people and draw them closer to you, Lord. Bring them healing, deliverance, salvation, and a closer walk with thee. Give me all that you want me to say in it. Give us favor today. Thank you for supplying all that I need.

Seek your face forevermore.

You're qualified.

Max a million.

# May 04

To hear you, to hear your instruction, to be close to you and feel your presence are all I need. To have your peace and joy, to feel your love, and to know that you are pleased with me is my desire. I want to know you more intimately and have your wisdom, might, and understanding. I want to fear the Lord, to walk in the Spirit at all times, and for my children and family to be close to you. I want to walk in the knowledge of your will and fulfill all that you have destined for me to do. I desire to seek you with all of my heart and be all that you have called me to be.

Give me the wisdom, courage, and strength to do your will and obey you. Lead me by the Holy Spirit. May I always be in your perfect will. May I always be a blessing to others. Thank you for blessing me to be a blessing every day of my life.

The richness of the Lord.

Watch and see what I will do.

"The wealth of the wicked is stored up for the righteous." Proverbs 13:22. "Righteousness exalts a nation." Proverbs 14:34.

"The path of the just is like the shining sun, that shines ever brighter unto the perfect day." Proverbs 4:18. Continuance.

Fill me to overflowing with your presence.

Stocks and bonds.

Majesty.

Winepress.

All is well, my darling

Much peace.

# MAY 07

Watch and pray. Help me to trust you in everything.

Litigation.

Much love. The best for the rest of my life.

A closer walk with thee.

To hear you, Lord, is my plea.

Leaning on everlasting arms. My love, my love, my love.

Worship the King.

Santo Domingo.

The depths of my love are unfathomable.

The minister of the Lord.

# MAY 10

Father, draw me close to you and lead me by your Holy Spirit. Help me to make wise choices in my life. Direct my steps and bring me to whom you would have help me in the promotion of this book. Bring me to the person who can assist me.

Bless our family, Lord.

I wait patiently for you. Speak through me. Thank you that I am every bit whole.

Our marriage is priceless and precious and blessed by you, Lord. Our house is filled with all pleasant riches. "The house of the uncompromisingly righteous shall flourish."

# MAY 14

Father, how can I ever express how grateful I am to you for my precious husband, children, grandchildren, and family? I love them so much. My life is truly complete and totally blessed by these precious gifts you have given me. As I look at my life, I realize how blessed I am. I am thankful that you protected me by giving me the family I was raised in. You have had your hand upon my life and caused me to have everlasting joy and peace by your blessings. My heart is overjoyed to know you, to have an intimate relationship with you, and to feel secure that you are taking care of me. Thank you for your blessings upon me and this family. Thank you for giving me favor with you and man.

Thank you for the success of our businesses. You are truly all that we need. It is you who have given us direction and favor. You go before me and help me in every decision. I seek your guidance. It is about you, not me.

The riches of the Lord. A place of peace.

Give my sister favor with this interview. May she seek you with her whole heart. Bring healing and restoration to her life. I know that she is in the palm of your hand. Encourage her today, and my husband also. Thank you for helping him and giving him favor in all that he does.

May I focus on what is in the heart and not on outside appearances.

It's a matter of the heart.

Pentecost: revival coming to us. Holy Ghost fire.

All to you I owe.

# MAY 16

I sing praises to your name. I seek you with my whole heart, o Lord. I pray that all men and women and children will seek you. May they forget what man thinks of them and desire only to know you—really know you, hear you, be led by you, and obey you. Let them long just to please you, not having the mere form of godliness but truly knowing you.

"Righteousness exalts a nation." Proverbs 14:34. Shun evil. Turn completely away from evil. May they seek purity and the cleanliness of your presence. May knowing you intimately be all that they desire. May they run to you and cling to you. You will lead them in the way of righteousness. Peace and joy will fill their lives.

This world needs you, Lord. Send revival to this land—a Pentecost revival. Wisdom, righteousness, sanctification, and redemption belong to us. Thank you, Father, for redeeming us. Worship the King.

"Draw near to me and I will draw near to you." James 4:8. The refreshing of the Lord, mind, spirit, and body.

"Come unto me, all you who labor are heavy laden, and I will give you rest. Take my yoke upon you and learn from me, for I am gentle and lowly in heart, and you will find rest for your souls. For my yoke is easy and my burden is light." Matthew 11:28-30.

Onward, Christian soldier.

Matchless name.

# MAY 21

Precious Lord,

Thank you for healing my arm. Thank you for giving me favor today and blessing this family and our businesses. Thank you for causing my husband to flourish and blessing us spiritually.

Thank you for the abundance of peace you have given me.

Thank you for my sister getting the job. I pray that she will love it and will be used as a blessing as well as being blessed in it.

Let my family know how much I love them. Let my husband know how very proud I am of him. Thank you for blessing me with him. He is such a wonderful gift from you. I adore him.

In all that you have planned for me, help me to obey, follow your lead, and stay on the path you have chosen. "Righteousness exalts a nation." Proverbs 14:34. "Blessings chase the righteous." Deuteronomy 28:2.

*Linda Walker*

# MAY 22

I will praise and glorify your name. Thank you for great peace and joy and contentment. Thank you for what you are doing with the book. Help me in all aspects of it. I give you glory for it.

You are the one who gave it all to me. Help me to bless all whom you would have me bless. Show me the path to walk, and I will follow and obey you. Riches and honor belong to us.

We are blessed to be a blessing. Draw near to me and I will draw near to you.

Onward, Christian soldier.

# MAY 23

There is great deliverance through praise.

Thank you for total restoration in this family. Thank you for giving us love and unity: one accord in favor and blessings. Righteousness, sanctification, redemption, and the fear of the Lord belong to us. Set my sister free from all fear, anxiety, and bondages. Draw her and my brother by your Holy Spirit closer to you.

Everlasting joy and gladness belong to us. Favor, peace, love, healing, deliverance, wisdom, joy, and righteousness belong to us. We receive them now. We receive provision and abundant life refreshing for both of us and complete fullness in you, enjoying our lives and loving each other more each day with the richness of the Lord.

Wash over us with your love.

Thank you for your goodness in the land of the living. Loving not my life until death.

# MAY 24

Thank you for blessing me to write this book. Thank you for causing it to be very successful. Thank you for causing many to be restored to you and have hope renewed in their lives.

"Mercy triumphs over judgment." James 2:13. Wonder of wonders for all you are doing in our lives.

Blessings overtake us. Bless the publishers. May they prosper and be exceedingly blessed.

I ask for favor and anointing upon the book. Bless all who read it. May they draw closer to you and their lives never be the same. In Jesus' name.

Household restoration.

"Mercy triumphs over judgment." James 2:13.

# MAY 25

Thank you, Lord, for household restoration and for our new home. Thank you for your presence and your loving peace. All of heaven's treasures are ours. Thank you for the songs you put in my heart last night. Thank you for your love and great peace. Thank you for my family and for my new beginning.

Watchman on the wall.

"Cast your bread upon the water;" Ecclesiastes 11:1. "Cast your care upon the Lord." 1Peter 5:7.

Riches and honor and wealth shall be in our house

Abundant provision, abundant supply.

Much prosperity, much peace, and the fear of the Lord.

# MAY 28

Thank you, Lord, for all of your promises and what you speak to me. Thank you for the plans and purposes that you have prepared for me. Thank you for your angels who are encamped around our family to minister and protect us daily. Reveal your will for me today. Give me favor, direction, blessings, courage, and strength. Thank you for healing me and for my joy.

Direct my steps today and help me to do all that you have planned for me to do.

Overflowing joy, overflowing peace, overflowing love, overflowing presence, overwhelming love, and overwhelming goodness.

Gorgeous.

# MAY 29

I know that you are taking me down the path you have already prepared for me.

Keep me as the apple of your eye. Keep me meek and humble, always trusting in your help. Let me express your heart and love to others. Let me encourage others and be in tune with your voice, knowing that you protect me and my family always. We walk in the blessings of the Lord.

Help me to help people come into your presence. Help them seek you at all times, worship you, and live whole and full of peace, joy, and love. Help them to be healed and blessed, spiritually, physically, and financially. May I seek you with all of my heart, to please you and you alone.

Thank you that our marriage is as days of heaven upon this earth. Our children and grandchildren will serve and love you all the days of their lives. Help me to be an example of you to this world. Help me to be steadfast and to excel in what you have called me to do. I honor you in all I say and do. I want to represent you to this world and be your light, succeeding in all you ask me to do for you.

"Mercy triumphs over judgment." James 2:13. Thank you for your mercy and love. Help me to do your perfect will for my life, and forgive me when I haven't. Perfect unity and love in our home and family are what you desire for us. I love others and forgive others and walk in peace. Go before me and behind me and give me all you want me to write in the messages. Holy Spirit, bring to my spirit all you would have me write.

Purpose-driven life.

Watchtower.

# JUNE

# June 01

Thank you for creating me to have fellowship with you. Thank you for keeping me on the path that you have designed for me. Thank you for the purpose that you created me for. Help me to listen and obey your leading. Thank you for this time of rest and refreshment in my life. Thank you for blessing our businesses. Thank you that our love grows stronger each and every day.

Mountain-moving faith.

The power of God.

Much richness, much abundance, much prosperity.

The best is yet to come!

The river of life. Abundance of peace and happiness.

At one with you, Lord.

Mountaintop experiences.

# June 05

Thank you, Father, for our son calling yesterday. Thank you for comforting me and being with me as I was at the dentist. Thank you for showing me my angel in a dream this morning.

Thank you that I am never alone. Your Holy Spirit is always with me, and your angels are encamped around me and my family. Thank you for blessing the work of our hands.

Thank you that you, in me, are the light of this world. Thank you for healing me. Thank you that your light shines brightly through me. Thank you for blessing my sister with a beautiful place.

I ask that many people be blessed by the magazine articles. All that you desire for me to do, you will help me to do. You will do it through me.

Highlight of the summer.

Thank you for setting me free from fear.

# June 06

*Six* means a double portion. Thank you, Father, for the double portion today. Double provision, double portion of healing, double portion of your goodness, double portion of your anointing, double portion of your presence, double portion of your favor, double portion of your wisdom, double portion of your mercy, and double portion of your revelations.

Double portion of your abundance. May your rich blessings shower upon us all, Lord.

Thank you for speaking to me and raining down your love upon me, Lord.

# June 08

I praise you, Lord, for my sister's new job. I pray that she will be a blessing. Help her to be excellent at her job and to reflect you. May she draw closer to you each and every day.

Great shall be the peace of our family. Thank you for my children and grandchildren.

Thank you for all the blessings that you have poured upon Fred and I. Thank you for the opportunity to enjoy and bask in the love you have filled our hearts with. Your presence in our lives is more precious than I can even express. Thank you for your peace, love, and joy.

Bless my husband today, and bless the work of his hands. Fill his heart and life with your love, peace, and presence today. Bless him for all the sacrifices he has made daily to serve this family, to bless us and many others.

A house of prayer.

"Righteousness exalts a nation." Proverbs 14:34.

Manifold grace of God.

Majesty, Majesty.

Reach out and touch someone.

Make me a blessing today.

# JUNE 09

Thank you, Father, for removing the sack cloth and ashes and putting on me the girdle of gladness, the robe of peace, and a frilly dancing dress. Thank you for healing my heart of sadness and sorrow and causing me to rejoice in the light of your presence and healing. Bring total restoration to this entire family.

I sing praises to your name. I worship you, Jehovah, for the abundance of blessings, for much fatness (anointing), and for richness in this land.

Much richness, much joy, much rejoicing, much prosperity.

Thank you for causing our marriage to be as days of heaven upon this earth. Everlasting joy and gladness is upon our heads. Thank you for making all things new just for you.

Washington, DC, victory campaign.

"May the Lord bless you.

May the Lord make his face shine upon you.

May the Lord be gracious to you.

May the Lord lift up his countenance upon you and give you peace." Numbers 6:24-26.

Much happiness.

# June 12

How I love to be in your presence. The day holds much busyness and much to do, but you always bless me. It is a blessing just to think about you throughout the day, knowing that you will help me and are with me. Your angels are encamped around me, protecting me. Thank you for filling me with your glory, your peace, your love, and your joy that overwhelms me.

I love to come and be in the secret place with you. I can hear you and be led by you and be comforted by you and receive direction from you. Reading your Word encourages me and builds my faith that you are in control of every area of my life.

This is my heart of love to you.

Pour out your Holy Spirit upon us. Bless us, such a blessing that there is not room enough to contain it all.

*Washington Post.*

The calling (of an apostle).

Richness of the Lord.

"Righteousness exalts a nation." Proverbs 14:34.

# JUNE 14

Father, I know that you see all and know all. Help me to be a better wife. Help me to honor my husband more and put his needs above others.

Thank you, Lord, for restoring all who read the book that is being published.

You are the sunshine of my love.

Much love, much happiness, much abundance, much prosperity, much joy, much peace, and much loving kindness.

Lover of my soul.

Spirit-transforming power.

Miraculous transformation.

Miracle-transforming power.

Miracle-transforming grace.

# JUNE 18

Thank you, Father, for overshadowing me, healing and restoring this family, and prospering and blessing us. Strengthen me. Give me your wisdom and lead me by your Holy Spirit. Help me to walk in love because love covers. Bless every person who reads the book.

Everlasting joy is upon our heads; riches are in our house.

"There is stability is in my times." Isaiah 33:6. You have given us all things richly to enjoy.

I bask in your love.

Holy, holy, holy is God Almighty. All the earth is filled with your glory.

Prosperity is my portion; wealth and the kingdom of God.

# June 19

Thank you for blessing me each day, Lord. Thank you for healing me. Thank you for my peace, joy, love, prosperity, and favor with you and man.

"Righteousness, peace, and joy in the Holy Ghost: that's the kingdom of God." Romans 14:17.

# June 20

Father, may the magazine articles bless many. May they draw closer to you as they read the articles. Thank you for all the abundance, love, joy, peace, grace, and fulfillment that comes from you.

A book of remembrance was written.

Riches shall be in our house. Much joy, much love, and much peace belong to us.

Thank you for wisdom from above.

Thank you for the gift of my husband. I praise you for him, and I love him.

I am guided by the Holy Spirit.

Much wealth, much prosperity, much abundance, much faithfulness, much gentleness, much gifting, and much soul searching, lover of my soul.

I am walking in the light as you are in the light, fulfilling my destiny to overflowing.

Walk in peace, walk in joy, walk in your love, walk in your presence, walk in your abundance, walk in fruitfulness, walk in your faithfulness.

A shiny new coat.

Thank you for the miracle of your grace.

The healing process has begun.

# JUNE 21

Thank you for miracles, signs, and wonders. Thank you, Father, for giving me peace yesterday at the dentist. Thank you for having Marilyn Hickey Ministries call last night for prayer just when I needed it. Thank you for healing me and for fresh manna today.

Thank you for restoration of this family and for blessing our business yesterday.

Many miracles. "Righteousness exalts a nation" Proverbs 14:34. ... Nationwide Insurance.

Much joy, much happiness, much peace belongs to me.

# June 22

"Righteousness exalts a nation." Proverbs 14:34.

"The fear of the Lord is the beginning of wisdom." Psalms 111:10.

Righteousness, sanctification, and redemption—blessed be the name of the Lord.

Much happiness, much joy, much love, much peace, much goodness, much gentleness, much prosperity, much abundance, much wisdom, much fear of the Lord, much graciousness.

Lord, thank you for the dream this morning. Thank you for letting me know that I have paid any balances that I might have owed my friend. My debt is paid off. I am now on my way, happy with my new journey and free. Thank you for releasing me and for the awesome plan you have for my life. I love you. I thank you for giving me freedom.

"Call to me, and I will answer you, and show you great and mighty things, which you do not know." Jeremiah 33:3.

Riches and honor, revelation, and the Word of God.

The supernatural presence of God.

Help me to be in your perfect will. Show us what you would have us do and how to be where you would have us be.

Matchless name.

Glory. Reveal your presence to us, Lord.

The manifested presence of God.

Thank you for your many blessings. Help us to be good stewards over all that you have given to us.

Rivers of living water. Rivers of love, pour upon us.

River of life, rain upon us. Rain down your love.

Manifest your love to me, overflowing, and wash away all the tears, the hurt, and the pain.

# June 27

Thank you, Lord, for washing clean all this land. Thank you for cleaning away filth and injustices and everything that needs to be cleansed. Forgive me for all my sins.

Cause my husband and I to be one in everything we do. We want to be a living sacrifice fit for the Master's use.

Wash me with your love. Protect us and fill us all with your glory, your loving kindness, and faithfulness, rightly divining the Word.

"O Magnify the Lord with me, and let us exalt his name together." Psalms 34:3. For the Lord is righteous.

Waves of mercy. Mercy triumphs over judgment.

Great peace have I given to you; focus on me.

"Blessed are the righteous. Their seed shall be mighty upon the earth. Wealth shall be in their house." Psalms 112:3.

Prince of Peace, I give you praise!

Matchless name.

Mighty God.

# June 28

When praises go up, blessings come down.

I will praise you with my whole heart. Thank you, Father, that you fill my heart and life with your glory. Thank you for the awesome plan and purpose you have for my life.

Thank you for rich blessings.

"O magnify the Lord with me and let us exalt his name together." Psalms 34:3. "Taste and see that the Lord is good; blessed is the man who trusts in him!" Psalms 34:8. "O give thanks to the Lord, for He is good! For his mercy endures forever." Psalms 118:1. Bless the Lord and praise His holy name.

Richness, healing, wisdom, righteousness, justice, mercy, goodness, faithfulness, abundance, prosperity, and greatness: you are all I need.

Wash over me with your love and fill me to overflowing.

Blessed to be a blessing, known to be known.

I want to please you. I want to be your bride, your fairest one, clothed in beautiful garments and smelling of your perfume. (Presence).

Strength and honor are my clothing. To do your will, o Lord, is my desire.

Matchless name.

Thank you for deliverance for this family and for renewing and refreshing us.

Thank you for the new thing that you are doing in my life, Lord, restoring all.

Abundant life: a life filled with all hope and peace and joy and gladness.

The richness of the Lord is all glorious within.

"Righteousness exalts a nation." Proverbs 14:34. In thirty days our debts shall be canceled. Thank you for our upcoming trip to Maui, all expenses paid. I declare this, In Jesus name.

Fill me to overflowing with your love, matchless love.

There are angels all around. Thank you for preparing us.

# JULY

# July 02

Thank you for the richness of the Lord.

Ties that bind.

Magnificent Father, full of wisdom and strength and favor.

# July 03

You are my refuge and strength. You will take care of us and all that is ours. You know what is best for us. You know every step I should take and every decision I should make. Lead us and help us, Lord. Keep unity and oneness and love in our family, I ask.

I know you will care for my children and grandchildren. May they know and understand that we love them. Help us to make wise choices in our lives. May we all trust you and seek your wisdom and guidance in every decision. You will lead us in the right path for the plans and purposes that you have for us.

Thank you that I am highly favored by you. "Righteousness exalts a nation." Proverbs 14:34.

Shine down your light upon us. "Mercy triumphs over judgment." James 2:13.

Radical change.

The holiness of God.

When praises go up, blessings come down.

March madness.

Engentel press.

# July 04

Thank you, Father, for telling me about Jerusalem, your city, city of peace that you want all of us to visit and be reminded of you. Help us to prepare to meet with you. You said your hand is upon your city night and day and that you protect it always. I pray for the peace of Jerusalem.

Thank you for your comfort today. Thank you that you always make a way for us. You always have a good plan for us, to prosper us and to give us peace and protection.

"Bless the Lord, O my soul; and all that is within me, bless his holy name

Bless the Lord O my soul, and forget not all His benefits;

Who forgives all of my iniquities, and who heals all of my diseases,

Who redeems your life from destruction,

Who crowns me with loving kindness and tender mercies,

Who satisfies my mouth with good things,

So that my youth is renewed like the eagles."

Bless the Lord, O my soul

Bless His Holy name. Psalms 103:1-5.

Bless all who read the book, Lord, and minister to them. Thank you for letting me speak to Cathy yesterday and for the card she mailed to me. How blessed I was.

Mark my word.

Thank you for joy unspeakable and full of your glory. Rest today.

Much peace, much joy, much abundance, much prosperity, much grace, much seed, much praise, the favor of God, goodness, richness, prosperity, and blessings.

# July 05

Thank you for always taking care of us and making a way for us. Thank you for the time I spend with you, basking in your presence and fellowshipping with you in your love.

Thank you for protection and provision for us. Great riches and honor belong to us.

You are my sunshine. You brighten my day and make a way where there seems no way.

"Wealth and riches shall be in our house." Psalms 112:3. Glory to your name.

A brave soldier.

"Great peace have those who love thy law, and nothing shall cause them to be offended." Psalms 119:165.

Come, sup with me.

Forever loved by you. "Mercy triumphs over judgment," James 2:13 my Prince of Peace, my bright and morning star.

Forever changed by your love and feasting on your presence.

Rightfully yours and understanding your promises.

Magnificent Jesus.

Watchman on the wall.

Right standing with you. Warrior.

Feasting at your table.

Every good and perfect gift comes from you.

Benefits of your love.

Go forward.

# JULY 06

Thank you for liberating me and setting me totally free. Free from trying to please anyone but you and only you. Thank you for my richly blessed, awesome life.

And filled with all of your goodness, gladness, hope, joy, peace, love, mercy, thankfulness, gentleness, glory, salvation, deliverance, healing, wholeness, prosperity, and richness in this life.

Kind heart, refreshing richness of the Lord, and the blessing of the Lord.

Love, loves.

# JULY 07

Father, forgive me of all my sins. Take away any impure thoughts and disobedience. Cleanse my heart. Purify my heart so that there are no hindrances between fellowshipping with your Holy Spirit. I must have a pure well flowing in me of clean fellowship with you. "Create in me a clean heart O God, and renew a right spirit within me. Do not cast me away from your presence, take not thy Holy Spirit from me." Psalms 51:10-11. Give me understanding of the prophetic edge.

How great thou art.

Brave heart.

Direct each of my steps and decisions concerning the book.

# JULY 09

Thank you, Lord, for your covenant with me and the promise of the Spirit.

Altogether lovely.

Forever yours.

Time spent with you is such a joyous time. Remove all evil from me and wash over me with your love.

Sweet fellowship.

"Mercy triumphs over judgment." James 2:13.

Rich revelation and rich abundance with the King.

Altogether lovely.

Wisdom, revelation, insight, and the fear of God.

Majesty on high, the Light of the World, righteous Judge, wash over us with your love, richness, and mercy.

Matchless name, Prince of Peace, a well springing up into everlasting life.

Righteous acts of the saints.

My favor, my darling.

Lord, thank you that the days of my captivity are over and all generational curses are now broken off from this family forever. In Jesus' name, by the blood of Jesus.

Thank you for revealing the future through your anointed prophets. Give them courage and give them peace and strength.

# July 11

Blessings chase us and overtake us. "Righteousness exalts a nation." Proverbs 14:34.

Thank you, Father, for your hand upon me.

Wisdom, ability, sanctification, and redemption. Thank you, Lord, that you will do the work through me. I am your helper, and you are my helper. Without you working through me, I can do nothing. It is you and your presence that everyone wants, not performance and not programs.

Forgive me for running after the gift that you have given to the people. It is you that we need.

I want your presence, the ministering and protection of your angels, and the Holy Spirit's presence in my life.

Watchtower. (Intercessor and prayer warrior).

Mountain on a hill, lover of my soul, and Light of the World.

March madness.

You are abundant in mercy. A radical change coming. Merciful Savior, shining bright.

Earth-shattering news.

# July 12

Wellsprings of life.

A permanent change is coming. Thank you, Lord, for total healing in me and this entire family. Thank you for your abundant favor and mercy and love.

Thank you for recording each of our days in a book and keeping it for eternity.

Thank you for the pressed-down, shaken-together, and running-over blessings in my life.

"I can do all things through Christ, who strengthens me." Philippians 4:13.

Exemplify.

Healing is thy portion. The cost was high, but I purchased it for you. Take and eat, Healing is the children's bread.

Tabernacle of praise, the fruit of my lips giving you praise.

Forever changed by the renewing of my mind.

Wellspring of life, renewing the mind of my beloved.

Ancient Israel.

This journey of my beloved.

Joy overflowing into wellsprings of life.

Manifold presence of God, tabernacle of praise.

All is well in my life.

This life of abundance and life of prosperity.

Blessings chase us and overtake us.

Glory, glory, glory, righteous Judge.

"But of Him you are in Christ Jesus, who became for us wisdom from God and righteousness and sanctification and redemption." (Wisdom, righteousness, sanctification, and redemption.) 1 Corinthians 1:30.

"And I can do all things through Christ, who strengthens me." Philippians 4:13.

My beloved.

"On Christ, the solid Rock, I stand; all other ground is sinking sand." {Edward Mote}.

*My Journey.*

# JULY 16

Thank you, Father, for a wonderful weekend. What happiness I have in my life.

Thank you for my husband and my family. I am so full of gladness and joy.

Show me each step of the way that you would have me to go.

Great riches, great peace, great love, great joy, great righteousness in the

Holy Ghost; that's the kingdom of God.

Ardent.

# July 17

Thank you, Lord, for my children, bless their marriages and their love and their families. Be strong in their marriages and in their lives every day.

"The blessing of the Lord makes one rich, and you add no sorrow with it." Proverbs 10:22. Thank you, Lord, that you always protect me and help me: demonstrating your love toward me, strengthening me, teaching me, and letting me know that I am to fear no man. You meet all of my needs. No one else can give me the love and peace that you do. Only you can give me the desires of my heart.

Our meeting place.

Let me love through you; let me help others through you.

Whistling pines. "Mercy triumphs over judgment." James 2:13.

Washington, DC. "Righteousness exalts a nation." Proverbs 14:34. Camp Mead.

"I seek first your kingdom, and all of these things shall be added to me."

*"My Journey."*

Much happiness, much joy, much peace, much love, much enjoyment. Wishing you prosperity, abundance, and favor.

"On Christ, the solid Rock, I stand; all other ground is sinking sand."

# July 18

Thank you, Lord, for our son Clint. What a joy our son is to us. Both of our sons are such a blessing to us. How you have filled our hearts with overflowing joy through the gifts of our children and grandchildren. They truly are gifts from you and are truly priceless to us.

Help me to obey you and be led by your Holy Spirit.

Blessings chase us and overtake us. Thank you for giving me favor at the book signings. May the books bless and help many, I ask.

"Mercy triumphs over judgment." James 2:13. Thank you for health and prosperity.

Juniper.

My heart's desire. "Delight yourself also in the Lord, and he shall give you the desires of your heart." Psalms 37:4.

# July 20

Thank you, Lord, for being in control of everything. You go before me and make the crooked places straight. Thank you for taking care of me. Give me peace and defeat my enemies. Heal me and forgive me, Lord.

Much joy, much peace, much happiness, much richness.

"Rock of ages cleft for me, let me hide myself in thee." {Augustus Montague Toplady}.

I am with thee. "The Lord is on my side; I will not fear; what can man do to me?" Psalms 118:6.

"Fear not, for I am with thee be not dismayed for I am your God." Isaiah 41:10." I will fear no evil; for you are with me; Thy rod and thy staff, they comfort me.

I prepare a table before thee in the presence of thy enemies. You anoint my head with oil; my cup runs over. Surely goodness and mercy shall follow me all the days of my life; and I will dwell in the house of the Lord forever." Psalms 23:4-6.

Father, help me with this message. Give me all you want me to say so that it may help others and draw them to you.

"Righteousness exalts a nation." Proverbs 14:34. Bring people back to you, Lord.

Holiness, righteousness, moral rectitude, and the fear of the Lord (reverence).

The divine presence of the Lord, a Holy Ghost revival.

I am with you always; I will never leave you.

I walk in wholeness.

Pulitzer Prize.

# July 21

Father, I want to follow hard after you. Keep me focused on what you would have me do. I know that you order my steps. I know that you love me and are directing me. Thank you for speaking to me last night. Comfort your grieving people who have lost loved ones.

One with you. My house is built on Jesus' love and righteousness. I stand on your solid foundation. You shall know the truth, and the truth shall make you free.

"Righteousness exalts a nation." Proverbs 14:34.

Matchless name.

The cove.

"Mercy triumphs over judgment." James 2:13.

# July 23

Father, I am so grateful that I have this time alone with you each day. I am grateful that you minister to me and give me words of comfort and love. Forgive me, Lord, for speaking evil against anyone or agreeing with any evil that has been told to me by others. Help me to think good of others. Help me to walk in love and unity and never speak evil of anyone. Help me to pray for those who make mistakes and have weaknesses. Help me to not rebel against any leadership in any area: work, home, or church. Forgive me when I have done this. Help me, Holy Spirit, to not judge or speak evil against any of your leadership, but to pray for them.

Envy and jealousy have no place in the lives of believers. We are to love one another and pray for one another.

Richness of your love.

You are the God of justice and mercy.

# July 24

Today is Mom's birthday. Happy birthday to my mom! She has been such a blessing to this family for all her life. She has loved us, taken care of all of us, and given to each of us all that we needed.

Mostly I praise you for the unconditional love that she has showered upon each of us all of our lives. She has never interfered with our families but has always been there to listen to us. I know she has prayed for us all of our lives.

Father, bless my mom. Give her comfort and joy today. Fill her life with your peace and love. May she live the rest of her days fulfilled in your love and presence.

Magna Carta.

Thank you for your loving kindness.

"O magnify the Lord with me, and let us exalt his name together." Psalms 34:3.

No one will be lost.

Covenant keepers. A lifetime of love.

Much love, much abundance, much prosperity, much joy, much peace.

Watchtower.

Free from fear. "Therefore if the son makes you free, you shall be free indeed." John 8:36.

Joy and gladness.

Boldness in the Lord.

# July 25

Father, I give you praise for all that you have done in my life. Thank you for teaching me your Word and for filling me with your Holy Spirit. Thank you for anointing me to do your will, for speaking to me, and for giving me dreams and visions. Thank you for blessing me with my husband and family. Thank you for filling my heart with your love and for being with me always. Thank you for giving me direction and also power over the enemy.

"Righteousness exalts a nation." Proverbs 14:34.

Thank you, Father, your Word gives me light, peace, joy, happiness, and goodness.

River of life, flow through me and manifest yourself in me.

What a privilege and honor to serve you, Lord. Wealth shall be in our house.

Thank you for your presence in my life, your tangible presence and your anointing.

Help me to do all that you would have me do. Lead me by your Holy Spirit to do your will, o Lord.

My Master, Savior, and Prince of Peace   I love you.

# JULY 26

I sing to you, Lord, and thank you from the bottom of my heart for all the good plans you have for me. Thank you for loving me always. Thank you for being with me in travel and in day-to-day life. Thank you for putting your light and glory in me, filling me with your love, peace, and joy.

Help me to write for the magazine the articles you would have me write. Bring those who read it closer to you, Lord. Help me in promoting the book. Give me favor with all. Give me what you would have me share. Help me to help them and give them hope, so they will grow closer to you. Help me to obey you and be faithful. I pray that they will see you. I walk as your representative, re-presenting you.

I heard the doorbell last night in my sleep. I knew it was you wanting to come in to our home and life. I opened the door this morning and welcomed you in.

# July 27

Father, thank you for speaking to me. Thank you for giving me dreams and visions and instruction in the way I should go. Forgive me for not wanting to fellowship with other believers. Help me to realize that you want us to fellowship together, help each other, and lift one another up. We were never meant to be alone in this world. We were created to fellowship with one another, and we need each other. Forgive me, Lord, for when I have wanted to be alone. Thank you for helping me to love others. Help me to reach out to them, accept them, and minister to them.

Thank you, Lord, for pouring out your glory cloud upon this family. I ask for the latter rain. Pour out your glory upon me and refresh me and our family so that I can refresh others who are dry and thirsty in this land. Refresh us, Lord, like the trees being refreshed by the rain, the grass sparkling, and the birds singing. Revive us again, Lord, and fill us to overflowing with your presence.

Holy Spirit, breath on us. Give us dreams and visions, direction and purpose.

Reveal to us our God-ordained purpose that you created us to do.

"Eye has not seen, nor ear has heard, nor have entered into the heart of man the things which God has prepared for those that love him." 1Corinthians 2:9.

Refinement.

# July 30

Father, thank you for being so real in my life. Thank you for your glory filling my life and my family. Thank you that your hand has held mine and helped me to make right choices.

Thank you for blessing me with my husband and family and filling my life with such fulfillment and joy. Because of your presence and guidance in my life, I feel so content and such peace.

Onward, Christian soldier. Rizpah. ( 2nd Samuel 21:10-14).

Enter in, my beloved.

Watchtower.

Love conquers all.

"By you I can run against a troop; and by my God I can leap over a wall." Psalms 18:29.

"Some trust in Chariots, and some trust in horses; but we will remember the name of the Lord our God." Psalms 20:7.

"Righteousness exalts a nation." Proverbs 14:34.

"But those who wait upon the Lord shall renew their strength; they shall mount up with wings like eagles; they shall run and not be weary, they shall walk and not faint." Isaiah 40:31.

Righteous one.

Exuberance.

Genuine Love. *Mizpeh* (watchtower).

*Mizpeh.*

# July 31

Thank you, Father, for speaking to me this morning. Thank you for our new home coming and for our new baby coming. Thank you for the book, Lord; give me favor with it.

Help me to be led by you more and more each day. Fill me with your praise all day.

# AUGUST

# August 01

"Bless the Lord, o my soul,

and all that is within me bless His holy name.

Bless the Lord, O my soul, and forget not all of His benefits, who forgives all of my iniquities, who heals all of my diseases, who redeems my life from destruction, who crowns me with loving kindness and tender mercies, who satisfies my mouth with good things, so that my youth is renewed like the eagle's."

"Bless the Lord o my soul and all that is within me Bless His holy name." Psalms 103:1-5.

Camp meeting.

Time with me is never wasted. Wichita, Kansas.

"Mercy triumphs over judgment." James 2:13.

Wonder of wonders. Thank you for anointing me to be me and not someone else. Thank you for blessing me to be a blessing.

Endeavor to do your best.

Righteous Judge.

Much happiness, much peace, much joy, much love, much abundance, much prosperity, much grace.

Make much of my presence.

Endeavor to do my will.

Righteous one.

"Blessed is the nation whose God is the Lord." Psalms 33:12.

Wrongful doing will be punished.

Much to do; go and do likewise.

# AUGUST 02

Father, thank you for your Word. Thank you for teaching me, for the teachers who have taught me, and for your Holy Spirit who teaches me. Thank you for my husband and for all that he does for me. Bless him, Lord, for being such a good husband and father. Give him the desires of his heart.

Direct my steps today, Lord, and help me make the decisions that you want me to make.

You make me to lie down in green pastures, and you restore my soul. Fill my heart with your Word.

"O magnify the Lord with me, and let us exalt his name together." Psalms 34:3.

"I dwell in a peaceable habitations and secure dwellings and in quiet resting places." Isaiah 32:18. And there is stability in my times. Isaiah 33:6.

Much joy, much happiness, much peace, much love, much harmony, much blessings, much abundance, much prosperity, much health, much longevity.

*Mizpah.* (Means watch Tower).

I walk in the blessing and the fullness of the Holy Spirit. Free to love and free to bless, free to minister and free to forgive. Free to live.

"He who the Son has set free is free indeed." John 8:36.

Maush.

# August 03

Yes, Father, I shall praise you. Even in the heavenly travels and where ever I go, I shall praise you. Praise defeats the Evil One and creates a pathway into your glory. I will praise you; it brings healing and health to me and to everyone else who does it. It beautifies me and causes me to look younger and brings peace to me. It drives the evil forces away.

Thank you, Lord, for what you are doing in this land today. You are greater than the evil in this world. Help me to be your light in this dark world. Help me to bring hope to others. Help me to learn your Word so I will have your wisdom. There is much to do. I am made in your image to represent you. I walk in your authority, power, and might.

Wisdom, sanctification, redemption, and the fear of the Lord. I put on love, I put on strength, and I walk in love. I go in confidence and in the fear of you, Lord.

# August 06

Thank you, Lord, for this brand-new day. Thank you for this brand-new way and for helping me take each step. Thank you for going before me and behind me and making the crooked places straight. Thank you for speaking November to me. We walk in your blessings, fulfilled in every way. Thank you for all the good things you have prepared for us. Help me in the next step. Give us favor in all we do, Lord. I apply your blood to my family.

Fear not, for I am with you. "My rod and my staff will comfort you. I prepare a table for you in the presence of your enemies. Thou anointest my head with oil; my cup runneth over. Surely goodness and mercy shall follow me all the days of my life." Psalms 23:4-6.

"Righteousness exalts a nation." Proverbs 14:34.

"Mercy triumphs over judgment." James 2:13.

Good things are coming my way, and a multitude of blessings unfolding.

Carry on, marsh.

Much happiness, much joy, much peace, much love, much fulfillment, much abundance, much longevity, much richness, much success. Rightful living, glorious living.

# AUGUST 07

Today is the day *My Journey* is released. Thank you, Lord, for giving me the book. I pray that the book will bless many and be very successful.

"Blessings chase the righteous and overtake them." Deuteronomy 28:2.

A wide door of opportunity has been opened to you.

Wonder of wonders.

Holy men of God.

Blessed by God, who always causes me to triumph. My help comes from the Lord, maker of heaven and earth. Heavenly bliss.

Mighty man of God (Fred).

Kingdom principles. (Thank you for the article for the magazine.)

# August 08

My journey home, my journey to you, Father. To be blessed, cleansed, and purified so that I can be a blessing to all you send me to.

My bright and morning star, lead me to you.

Keep my eyes upon you at all times. Much happiness, much peace, much love, and much contentment.

Bright and morning star is who you are. Lover of my soul works righteousness.

King of Kings and Lord of Lords, my strong tower clothed in righteousness and crowned in glory.

Righteous acts of the saints.

Wisdom, righteousness, sanctification, redemption, and the presence of the Lord.

Holy are you, Lord, and worthy to be praised. My Maker, my Master, my King,

Speak; your servant is listening.

# August 09

Thank you, Lord that you teach us to decree a thing and it shall be established. Give to me what you want me to say, and I will decree it.

Thank you, Father, for opening up the windows of heaven and pouring us out such blessings that we don't have room enough to receive them all. "(Bring all the tithes into the storehouse, that there may be food in my house, and try me now in this, says the lord of hosts, If I will not open for you the windows of heaven and pour out for you such blessing that there will not be room enough to receive it)."

Thank you for our health and my family's health. Protect us all.

Righteous acts of the saints. Help me to fulfill all of your will. Forgive me of all of my sins and wash me clean.

A Wide door of opportunity.

Much joy, much peace, much prosperity, much abundance, much love, much happiness, much contentment, and much longevity.

Endeavor to do your best.

# AUGUST 10

Thank you, Lord, for always taking such good care of me. Thank you for always protecting me and helping me and blessing me.

"Blessings chase the righteous and overtake us." Deuteronomy 28:2.

You are my firm foundation   love covers.

Fruitfulness and acceptance.

Thank you for the counsel and advice of my good friend.

How great thou art, magnificent Master.

Marsh.

# August 13

Lead me this day and help me to follow your every lead. Thank you for healing me and for your presence, your word and your wisdom, and for your favor.

Life as I have known it will never be the same. Put your hedge of protection around this family, Lord. Speak to them and guide them. May they seek you with all of their hearts and may they fulfill their destinies and callings.

Thank you for my brand-new beginning. May all who read the book grow closer to you, Lord.

Minister to them, heal them, and bless them. Thank you for your goodness.

Give to Fred and I a blessed, restful, and joyful anniversary.

With you all things are possible. "(If you can believe, all things are possible to him who believes.)" Mark 9:23.

Blessings chase us and overtake us. Thank you for our new home coming, Lord.

Thank you for much happiness. My desire is to hear your words of comfort, love, direction, and fellowship.

Much-needed rest.

Onward, Christian soldier.

# August 14

Thank you for my children and grandchildren. Protect them and minister to them. I declare that my children and grandchildren will serve you and worship you all the days of their lives. "All my children shall be taught by the Lord, and great shall be the peace of my children." Isaiah 54:13.

*Washington Post.*

You direct my steps, and we lack no good thing. "The young lions lack and suffer hunger, but those who seek the Lord shall not lack any good thing." Psalms 34:10.

A song of praise brings your angels to open our hearts to receive your Word. A song of praise and worship seals that Word in our hearts.

May I seek you first and always and know you intimately.

And by your stripes I am healed.

Accomplish much. "Righteousness exalts a nation." Proverbs 14:34.

"May the God of all grace, who called us to his eternal glory by Christ Jesus, after you have suffered a while, perfect, establish, strengthen, and settle you" minister to you and help you and encourage you and uplift you in every way. 1 Peter 5:10.

May your heart be filled with his praise.

"Our Father in heaven, hallowed be your name.

Thy kingdom come. Thy will be done, on earth as it is in heaven. Give us this day our daily bread. And forgive us our debts, as we forgive our debtors. And do not lead us into temptation, but deliver us from the evil one." Matthew 6:10-13.

"By you I can run through a troop, and by you I can leap over a wall." Psalms 18:29.

Forever changed in your presence.

Ancient ruins—we will rebuild the old waste places, and rebuild the city.

Marsh.

Whispering pines, the old winepress making a melody in my heart to the Lord.

"Come unto me, all you who labor and are heavy laden, and I will give you rest. Take my yoke upon you and learn from me, for I am gentle and lowly in heart, and you will find rest for your souls. For my yoke is easy and my burden is light." Matthew 11:28-30.

Come bask in my love.

"No good thing will you withhold from them that walk uprightly." Psalms 84:11.

Forever changed.

Walk in the light that you have.

All is well.

You are in my care.

# AUGUST 15

March madness.

"Peace I leave with you; my peace I give to you; not as the world gives do I give to you. Let not your heart be troubled, neither let it be afraid." John 14:27.

Much happiness, much peace, much love, much wisdom, much anointing, much treasure, much abundance, much prosperity, much magnification.

Capacity for more.

Wonder of wonders, capacity to do more.

Windsor Castle.

Fundamental breakthrough. Righteous acts of the saints.

Prosperity cometh to me now. Abundant riches, cascading waterfalls, and rolling hills.

Fundamentally sound.

Magnificent one, captivate my heart.

Winds of change are blowing.

Catapult me to the next level.

Jehovah Tsidkenu—the Lord, my righteousness. Your banner over me is love.

Abundant mercy, overpowering love, abundant grace and goodness.

Mercy of the Lord, crowned with loving kindness and tender mercies.

Watchtower.

Wash over me with your love. My light goes forth and shines in the darkness, setting the captives free. Many will be healed; many will be blessed.

Marvelous are your ways.

Time sensitive. Quiet your heart with my word and be sensitive to the movement of the Holy Spirit.

Fulfill your calling. Live life to the fullest, making disciples of all men and setting the captives free. Baptize them in the name of the Father, the Son, and the Holy Ghost.

Endeavor to do your best.

Who will ascend to your holy hill? Those who have clean hands and a pure heart.

# AUGUST 16

Lead me to do all you would have me do each day, Lord. Direct my steps. Help me to live a life of highest integrity and represent you as light to this dark world. Lead me, Holy Spirit, to do what is good, just, noble, and of right character. May others turn to you, repent of their sins, and choose to live for you. May they be filled with your awesome presence.

"My peace I leave with you, my peace I give to you; not as the world gives do I give to you. Let not your heart be troubled, neither let it be afraid." John 14:27.

"Blessed is the nation whose God is the Lord." Psalms 33:12.

Stockpile.

All that the Lord is speaking to me in my spirit is what He wants me to share with the world. He speaks to us, his children. We listen to his instruction, his comforting words, and his love to us.

Blessed be the Lord who always causes me to triumph. Minister to me your perfect will. Much love upon the earth engrafted into Him.

His wisdom, his knowledge, his righteousness, his redemption, his sanctification on those set apart.

Walking close by your side, my Master, my Savior, my Prince of Peace, my strong tower. The righteous run into it and they are safe.

Come, my darling. Manifest your presence in my life. Take my yoke upon you and learn of me, for my yoke is easy and my burden is light.

"Blessed are the Righteous His descendants will be mighty on earth; the generation of the upright will be blessed. Wealth and riches will be in his house and his righteousness endures forever." Psalms 112:1-3.

Multiplied, multiplied by tens of thousands.

I walk in the favor of God. Much joy, much prosperity, much abundance, much peace, much love, much wisdom, and much righteousness.

"Whispering Pines."

Your still, small voice—come, Holy Spirit; make your presence known.

The sky's the limit. The righteous acts of the saints.

Prayer warrior.

Watch and see what I am going to do.

# AUGUST 21

The lover of my soul, watch and pray. Seek my face. Turn from your wicked ways, and I will forgive your sins and heal your land.

I ask you for wisdom today, Lord. Seek me with all of your heart.

"Mercy triumphs over judgment." James 2:13. The manifold presence of God; righteous acts of the saints.

*Washington Post.*

Fill me to overflowing with your Word, Holy Spirit and the presence of the Lord.

Overwhelming love.

Help me speak only what you want me to say. Help me to say what you want to come to pass in my life. Righteous acts of the saints.

Minister to me. I know you will take care of everything that we have need of.

Minister. Whispering pines.

Much joy, much happiness, much love, much fruit, much abundance, much prosperity.

My restorer of life. With long life I satisfy you and show you my salvation.

Much-needed rest. Lover of my soul, lean on me. "Restore unto me the joy of thy salvation and renew a right spirit within me, uphold me by your generous Spirit."

"Hope thou in me." Psalms 42:11.

"Bless the Lord, o my soul, and all that is within me bless His holy name.

Bless the Lord, O my soul, and forget not all of His benefits. Who forgives all of your iniquities, who heals all of your diseases, who redeems your life from destruction, who crowns you with loving kindness and tender mercies, Who satisfies my mouth with good things so that my youth is renewed like the eagle's."

Bless the Lord, o my soul; and all that is within me, Bless His holy name. Psalm 103:1

"Righteousness exalts a nation." Proverbs 14:34.

# AUGUST 22

How awesome to have this time with you in your presence. I know that you know the desires of our hearts. You meet every need that we have according to your will. I worship you, Lord. With an outstretched arm you came to seek and to save those who are lost. You want the best for each of us.

Give me your wisdom to know how to give an answer to them in due season.

I love and honor you, Lord. Blessings chase us and overtake us. "The weapons of our warfare are not carnal but mighty in God for pulling down of strongholds, casting down imaginations (arguments) and every high thing that exalts itself against the knowledge of God, and bringing every thought captive to the obedience of Christ."2Corinthians 10:4-5.

Thank you, Lord that our warfare is not with flesh and blood but with principalities and powers and wickedness (the Enemy). I put on the full armor of God, and I know that your angels are protecting me and my family. Richness in life: much abundance, much prosperity, much peace, much love.

"Cast all of your care upon me, for I care for you." 1 Peter 5:7.

# August 23

My servant, my love, my ever-present help in time of need. Sweet psalmist of Israel, my high tower: I run into it and I am safe. You make all the rough places straight.

"Lily of the valley, bright and morning star you are." {Charles W. Fry}.

Much happiness, much peace, much loving kindness.

All the former things have passed away, and behold, I will do a new thing. Now shall you not see it? "Behold, I will do a new thing, now it shall spring forth shall you not know it?"

"I will even make a road in the wilderness and rivers in the desert." Isaiah 43:19. "For I will pour water on him who is thirsty, and floods on the dry ground; I will pour my Spirit on your descendants, and my blessing on your offspring." Isaiah 44:3. "There is a river whose streams make glad the city of God." Psalms 46:4. Angel of light: that is who you are.

"Whispering Pines."

You are my angel of light. Jesus Christ, "the same yesterday, today, and forever," Hebrews 13:8. Light of the World. *Mizpeh.* (Watchtower.)

Rest in my love. Thank you, Lord, for blessing our marriage for thirty-seven years today.

Continue to bless us, Lord. May our love grow stronger and stronger each day with love and peace. Matchless love and peace.

"For the weapons of our warfare are not carnal but mighty in God for the pulling down of strongholds." 2 Corinthians 10:4.

*Linda Walker*

Your love is shed abroad in my heart by the Holy Spirit. "Now hope does not disappoint, because the love of God has been poured out in our hearts by the Holy Spirit who was given to us." Romans 5:5. Much to do.

Ample time. Ever-increasing faith. Much happiness, much peace, much joy, much love. The joy of the Lord is my strength for all to see. Multiplied by thousands of souls.

Onward, Christian soldier. There is a purpose. Make glad the city.

Watchman on the wall.

# August 24

Matchless name. Forward. Much happiness, much love. "Whispering Pines."

Ever-increasing faith. "By your stripes I am healed." 1 Peter 2:24. "Blessed is the man who fears the Lord, who delights greatly in his commandments. His descendants will be mighty on earth; the generation of the upright will be blessed. Wealth and riches will be in his house and his righteousness endures forever." Psalms 112:1-3.

Prosperity, abundance, and the fear of the Lord. Much-needed rest.

Occupy until I come.

From the rising of the sun to the going down of the same, great is your name and greatly to be praised.

Enlightenment   richness of the Lord.

"Surely blessing I will bless you; and multiplying I will multiply you." Hebrews 6:14. In this land you shall possess double wealth. Riches shall be in our house. The house of the uncompromisingly righteous flourishes. "Therefore in their land they shall possess double; and everlasting joy shall be upon their heads." Isaiah 61:7.

Prince of Peace, righteous one.

With man this is impossible, "but with God all things are possible." Matthew 19:26. Cultivate a lifestyle of praise.

*Mekadesh* (The Lord who sanctifies).

"From the rising of the sun to its going down the Lord's name is to be praised." Great is the Lord and greatly to be praised, bless His holy name. Psalms 113:3.

Melchizedek the priest.

Bright and morning star.

Unspeakable joy. Onward, Christian soldier.

Blood of the sacrifice: Jesus.

Great is your name and greatly to be praised.

Bought with a price; abide in my love. Blessings chase us and overtake us.

(Wuthering Heights.)

Much happiness, much joy, much peace.

(March madness.)

# AUGUST 28

Father, I want to live in your presence every day of my life. Fill me to overflowing with your glory. My desire is to be in your courts daily, fellowshipping with you and in your glory.

Speak to me, Lord. Direct my steps and life.

Thank you for wisdom from above.

National and international.

Living in your presence; fulfilling your call.

Mekadesh. (The Lord who sanctifies.)

Richness of the Lord, my glory.

All is well.

Leaning on the everlasting arms, I go in the fear of the Lord.

Onward, Christian soldier.

# AUGUST 30

Help me to reflect you, Lord, in all I do and in all I say. Bring unity into this nation and character and integrity into this country. Draw people back to you, Lord. This land is a Christian nation. Blow your winds of change and bring revival into this land now, I ask. Multiple times multiple of souls into your kingdom, I ask, Father: tens of thousands.

Reach out and touch someone.

*Mizpah* (watchtower).

Righteousness exalts a nation.

# AUGUST 31

Thank you, Lord, for a covenant sign between me and you. Thank you for letting me know your will. Fulfill all you've promised me. You shall bless this family, and we shall praise your name and give you all the glory in Jesus' name. You go before me and open doors for me. I praise your name. (Whispering pines).

Great peace have I given you; "peace I leave with you, my peace I give to you; not as the world gives do I give to you. Let not your heart be troubled; neither let it be afraid." John 14:27.

"Not forsaking the assembling of ourselves together, as in the manner of some, but exhorting one another, and so much the more as you see the day approaching." Hebrews 10:25. Wash us by the washing of your Word. ("That he might sanctify and cleanse her with the washing of water by the word.")

Genuine love.

I call upon the name of the Lord, who made heaven and earth.

Watchtower. "Mercy triumphs over judgment." James 2:13.

*Mizpah.* (Watchtower.) "Whispering Pines."

*Washington Post.*

Unfailing love, tender heart.

Blessed Redeemer, the Savior is mine.

Divine purpose, Light of the World.

Matchless name.

Endeavor to do your best. Minister.

Richness of the Lord. A time for all to see.

# SEPTEMBER

# September 04

The stillness of the Lord. I hear the voice of the Shepherd, and the voice of a stranger I will not follow. ("Yet they will by no means follow a stranger, but will flee from him, for they do not know the voice of strangers." John 10:5. "My sheep hear my voice, and I know them, and they follow me.")v 27. Much happiness, much peace, much love, much intimacy. My strong tower. Matchless name. Enjoy the company. Wonder of wonders.

Decently and in order (the book signings).

Pentecostal fires.

Much-needed rest; restore my soul to rest in peace.

Healing is thy portion. Let not your heart be troubled; neither let it be afraid.

The giver of light, "Prince of Peace, bright and morning star," you are.

Lover of my soul, blessed Redeemer, Majesty on high.

Clear to hear.

Much happiness, much joy, much peace, much love, much contentment.

Righteous King, my rewarder.

"And you seek me and find me, when you search for me with all your heart." Jeremiah 29:13. "The young lions lack and suffer hunger; but those who seek the Lord shall not lack any good thing." Psalms 34:10.

Preserver of life.

Glory to the Lord. Thank you, Lord that I am in covenant with you and for the covenant you made with Abraham. It is for all of his seed. Thank you that you never break this covenant. Thank you for my marriage covenant; it is never to be broken. Thank you that we are under the blessings of the Lord and no evil will befall me or my family.

(March madness.)

You became for me wisdom, righteousness, sanctification, and redemption. Manifest yourself to me, Lord, from on high, from your holy hill.

"Many are the afflictions of the righteous, but the Lord delivers him out of them all." Psalms 34:19.

Bright and shining star, hedge of protection you are. Much wealth, much riches, much abundance. The favor of the Lord: crown of life, riches, and honor.

"The fear of the Lord is the beginning of wisdom; a good understanding have all those who do his commandments." Psalms 111:10.

Obedience. Abundance of peace.

Onward, Christian soldier.

# SEPTEMBER 06

Blessings chase us and overtake us. "Surely goodness and mercy shall follow me all the days of my life; and I will dwell in the house of the lord forever." Psalms 23:6.

Favorable conditions. Much abundance, much prosperity, much peace, much joy, much love.

Richness of the Lord, my high tower.

Much loveliness.

"Righteousness exalts a nation." Proverbs 14:34. "My hope is built on nothing less than Jesus blood and his righteousness." {Edward Mote}. "Hope deferred makes the heart sick." Proverbs 13:12. My Rock, my strong tower: "the name of the Lord is a strong tower; the righteous run into it and are safe." Proverbs 18:10.

The yoke-destroying, burden-removing power of God. ("It shall come to pass in that day that his burden will be taken away from your shoulder, and his yoke from your neck and the yoke will be destroyed because of the anointing oil.") Isaiah 10:27.

"Mercy triumphs over judgment." James 2:13.

In your presence is fullness of joy. Watchtower.

Right standing with God exalts a nation.

Peaceful praise.

One nation under God. Maush.

# SEPTEMBER 07

Thank you, Father that you gave us your Son and put on Him all of our sins, sicknesses, condemnation, and everything else that the world tries to put on us. When others try to put guilt and condemnation on us, your children, you take those upon yourself. We are in the Spirit. You give us life and peace without any guilt. I walk in the Spirit, not in the flesh.

"There is therefore now no condemnation to those who are in Christ Jesus, who do not walk according to the flesh, but according to the Spirit." (Romans 8:1).

Thank you that I walk in the Spirit, so I walk in life and peace. Thank you for your blood that cleanses me from all unrighteousness. Thank you for the mercy seat. "Mercy and truth have met together; Righteousness and peace have kissed. "Psalms 85:10. I walk and dwell in your unconditional love and acceptance.

Thank you that you accept me and I am accepted in the beloved." To the praise of the glory of his grace, by which he made us accepted in the beloved.") Ephesians 1:6. Thank you for ministering to me today. Father, I am your child.

"Great peace have those who love thy law, and nothing shall cause them to be offended." Psalm 119:165.

I love your word, Lord. It gives me wisdom, deliverance, peace, and life. The anointing destroys every yoke and removes every burden in people's lives.

It is the yoke-destroying, burden-removing power of God. ("That his burden will be taken away from your shoulder, and his yoke from your neck and the yoke will be destroyed because of the anointing oil.") Isaiah 10:27. I walk in newness of life. I am clothed in your love and the joy of the Lord. "Sorrow and sighing have fled away from me." Isaiah 35:10. Thank you for setting me free from all my guilt and shame and fear. Blessed be my Lord.

Run, river, run. Wash over me with your love.

Love never condemns. I go in peace.


# SEPTEMBER 08

Thank you for this day, a day of celebration, a day that will give hope and encouragement in the lives of all who want it. Thank you for blessing me to be your instrument of praise and adoration to a hurting and confused world. Help me today, Holy Spirit, to speak what you would have me speak. Give me your wisdom, healing, and favor. Make me a blessing today in the lives of your people.

Much happiness, much love, much peace, much fellowship, much celebration, much joy.

All your billows wash over me with your love and presence.

Reach out and touch someone. Matchless name, ancient of days.

Prosperity shall follow; "the name of the Lord is a strong tower; the righteous will run to it and shall be safe." Proverbs 18:10.

Prosperity will come.

Endeavor to do your best.

Righteous acts of the saints.

# September 10

Rock-solid faith, pursue peace and righteousness. Without it, no one will see the Lord.

March madness.

I pray for the peace of this nation: one nation under God. Righteous acts of the saints.

"Our Father in heaven, hallowed by your name, Thy kingdom come, thy will be done, on earth as it is in heaven. Give us this day our daily bread, and forgive us our debts, as we forgive our debtors. And lead us not into temptation, but deliver us from evil, for thine is the kingdom, the power, and the glory forever." Amen. Matthew 6:10-13.

Righteous one, love forgives. "Love suffers long and is kind; love does not envy; love does not parade itself, is not puffed up; does not behave rudely, does not seek its own, is not provoked, thinks no evil; does not rejoice in iniquity, but rejoices in the truth. It keeps no record of wrongs, bears all things, believes all things, hopes all things, endures all things, Love never fails." 1 Corinthians 13:4-8.

Much abundance and peace. Duty calls, much to do.

Do not cast your figs before their time. "Therefore humble yourselves under the mighty hand of God, that he may exalt you in due time." 1 Peter 5:6. "Trust in the Lord with all your heart, and lean not on your own understanding; in all your ways, acknowledge him and he shall direct your paths." Proverbs3:5-6.

The Prince of Peace will not break the covenant of peace.

Morning star you are.

"Come, Holy Spirit, sweet heavenly dove. Stay right here with us, filling us with your love. For these blessings, we lift our hearts. We say without a doubt we know that we have been revived when we leave this place." {Doris Mae Akers}.

King of Kings, Lord of Lords, bright and morning star, magnificent Savior, the great I Am.

No one can compare to you, Holy One. No other name will ever reign in glory and power.

Sing to the Lord with your whole heart; sing praises to his name.

I stand in awe of you, Holy God, to whom all praise is due. I stand in awe of you.

Come into my holy presence. Worship the King. Freedom reigns. I'm free, I'm free; my God has set me free.

"Therefore if the son makes you free, you shall be free indeed." John 8:36. "And I also say to you that you are Peter, and on this rock I will build my church, and the gates of hell will not prevail against it." Matthew 16:18. My glorious church, saints of all nations.

Much joy and peace, much love and forgiveness, much favor and abundance.

One nation under God and deliverance for all. I partake of all your goodness for all time.

"The generation of the upright shall be blessed." Psalms 112:2. Abundance for all and for all I say good night.

# September 11

Comfort all who mourn today, Lord, and give them your peace. May they feel your love.

(March madness.) Comfort those in Zion.

Without you I can do nothing, but with you all things are possible. ("I am the vine, you are the branches. He who abides in me, and I in him, bears much fruit; for without me you can do nothing." John 15:5 One Nation under God, with liberty and justice for all.

Eternal Rock.

Give us, Lord, a time to love, a time to dance, a time to be fulfilled, and a time of purpose.

Much happiness, much peace, much joy, and much love.

Thank you for your love letter to me. Thank you that I can write my love letters to you.

Complete joy, completely enthralled in your love, the lover of my soul.

Rise up and fulfill your calling. Go forth in my power and authority. Fulfill your destiny and purpose and high calling of the Lord.

## September 12

Thank you for sunshine and light. Thank you for your protection and for your angels ministering to us. Help me to fulfill all that you have called me to do to be a blessing to all you put me around. Matters of the heart. (Thank you for giving to me my next article).

Deluge. "Create in me a clean heart, O God, and renew a steadfast spirit within me. Do not cast me away from your presence, and do not take your Holy Spirit from me." Psalms 51:10-11.

I seek you for your direction. Help me to make the choices that you have for me, your perfect will for my life.

"Blessed are the peacemakers, for they shall be called sons of God." Matthew 5:9.

## September 13

Thank you, Father, for the promises of the covenant that belongs to me and my family.

Thank you that you want me to be blessed with lands, prosperity, riches, nice houses, and material things. You provide and take care of me. You want me to have peace, rest, riches, honor, and a long, fulfilled life.

"The generation of the upright will be blessed. Wealth and riches will be in his house, and his righteousness endures forever." Psalms 112:2-3. Prosperity and riches belong to us. "Wisdom and knowledge will be the stability of your times, and the strength of salvation; the fear of the lord is his treasure." Isaiah 33:6. "Depart from evil and do good; seek peace and pursue it." 1 Peter 3:11. We seek peace and pursue it.

# SEPTEMBER 14

Thank you, Father, for anointing me with fresh oil for the new thing you are doing in my life.

Much happiness, much peace, much love, and much joy belong to me.

Thank you, Lord, for giving me all the dreams and visions. Thank you for the prayers that have been prayed over me. Much quietness and assurance. Pursue peace with all people, and holiness, without which no one will see the Lord.

All my billows wash over you with love. Pleasant.

Occupy until I come. Great abundance, great joy, and great peace.

Followers of Christ. Maker of heaven and earth. Righteous Judge and Prince of Peace is who you are. "Every good gift and every perfect gift comes from above, and comes down from the Father of lights, with whom there is no variation or shadow of turning."

"Thy kingdom come, thy will be done, on earth as it is in heaven." Matthew 6:10. "You will show me the path of life; in your presence is fullness of joy, and at thy right hand are pleasures forevermore." Psalms 16:11.

Come, my beloved. Let us take counsel together amid a wicked and perverse nation.

"Righteousness exalts a nation." Proverbs 14:34. "Let them shout for joy and be glad, who favor my righteous cause; let the Lord be magnified who has pleasure in the prosperity of his servant." Psalms 35:27. Come and dine with me. "There is no fear in love but perfect love cast out all fear, because fear involves torment. But he who fears has not been made perfect in love." 1 John 4:18. Truly I say to you, "unless the lord builds the house, they labor in vain who build it." Psalms 127:1. " My hope is built on nothing less than Jesus' blood and righteousness.

On Christ, the solid Rock, I stand. All other ground is sinking sand." {Edward Mote}. Carry on.

"Now may the God of peace himself sanctify you completely; and may your whole spirit, soul, and body be preserved blameless at the coming of our lord Jesus Christ." 1 Thessalonians 5:23. Matchless name and righteous one. A glimmer of hope. Rock-solid faith.

## September 17

Father, thank you for the opportunity to minister and visit with your people at the book store and book signing. Bless all who purchased the book and minister to them who read it.

Thank you for the quiet time I have to spend in your presence, hearing from you, talking with you, and listening to your voice. "My sheep hear my voice, and I know them, and they follow me." John 10:27. And a stranger they will not follow. "And I heard a voice from heaven, like the voice of many waters, and like the voice of loud thunder." Revelation 14:2.

The voice of many waters, speak. Your servant is listening. Ruark.

Whistling pines. "Who made heaven and earth, the sea, and all that is them; who keeps truth forever." Psalms 146:6. Enjoy my presence.

"But of him you are in Christ Jesus, who became for us Wisdom from God and righteousness and sanctification, and redemption." 1 Corinthians 1:30. Time alone with you is time well spent.

Like rivers of living water. "Oh, magnify the Lord with me, and let us exalt his name together." Psalms 34:3. Wash over me with your love. Called, anointed, and appointed to do my will. Blessed and honored to serve you.

# SEPTEMBER 18

You are in control of everything. I do not need to be concerned or worried or fretful about anything. I thank you, Lord, that you are mighty. I can bring all of my concerns to you and you will carry them for me. "And we know that all things work together for good to those who love God, to those who are the called according to his purpose." Romans 8:28.

All things work together for my good and for the purpose that you have called me for. Help me to fulfill that purpose. Guide me by the Holy Spirit to be a blessing to all you send me to. Help me to focus on doing your will and being pleasing to you, Lord.

"Not by might, nor by power, but by my Spirit says the Lord of hosts." Zechariah 4:6. "You will show me the path of life; in your presence is fullness of joy; at your right hand there are pleasures forevermore." Psalms 16:11. "By your stripes I am healed." 1 Peter

2:24. Prince of Peace is who you are. You rule in righteousness, our righteous Judge.

"Cast your bread upon the water and it will return to you not in many days." Ecclesiastes 11:1. "Blow the trumpet in Zion, consecrate a fast, call a sacred assembly; gather the people, sanctify the congregation, assemble the elders, gather the children and nursing babes; let the bridegroom go out from his chamber, and the bride from her dressing room." (Joel 2:15-16.

"I will say of the Lord he is my refuge and my fortress my god, in him I will trust." Psalms 91:2. "Blessed is the nation whose God is the Lord." Psalms 33:12.

My path is the path of righteousness. Come, Lord Jesus; heal this land.

"Righteousness exalts a nation." Proverbs 14:34. Our God reigns in the midst of a wicked and sinful nation.

Blessed by my God.

Richness of the Lord. Overcoming grace. Much grace and provision. Bedrock faith, forever changed into your image. Mountain-moving faith. "For the mountains shall depart and the hills be removed, but my kindness shall not depart from you, nor shall my covenant of peace be removed," says the Lord who has mercy on you." Isaiah 54:10.

"Jesus, Jesus, how I trust you. How I prove you more and more, Jesus, Jesus, precious Jesus.

O for grace to trust you more." {Louisa M. Stead}.

"Lead me, Lord, by your right hand. Lead me to the Promised Land. Lead me to your perfect plan. Lead me, Lord. Lead me, Lord, on this land by which I stand."

Fellowship, o Lord, with thee. Come away and be with me. Righteous Judge, I count on thee.

# SEPTEMBER 21

O how I love the Lord. Thank you that you take sickness away from the midst of me. Thank you that "mercy triumphs over judgment." James 2:13. "For all have sinned and fall short of the glory of God." Romans 3:23. Thank you for making my path straight and for making the rough places smooth.

"The crooked places shall be made straight and the rough ways smooth." Isaiah 40:4.

"Righteousness exalts a nation." Proverbs 14:34.

Come away with me, my love. "Blessed is the man who fears the lord, who delights greatly in his commandments. His descendants will be mighty on earth; the generation of the upright will be blessed. Wealth and riches will be in his house." Psalms 112:1-3. "The fear of God is the beginning of wisdom." Psalms 111:10. Blessed be my Rock, who always caused me to triumph. Ministry of reconciliation. ("Now all things are of God, who has reconciled us to himself through Jesus Christ, and has given us the ministry of reconciliation.") 1 Corinthians 5:18.

Righteousness triumphs over evil. "But those who wait on the Lord shall renew their strength; they shall mount up with wings like eagles, they shall run and not be weary, they shall walk and not faint." Isaiah 40:31.

"Great peace have those who love thy law and nothing shall cause them to stumble or be offended." Psalms 119:165. "Great is thy faithfulness," O Lord. {Thomas Obediah Chisholm}.

Nothing shall separate me from your love. Life, abundant grace, much peace and happiness. The fear of the Lord is the beginning of wisdom. Righteousness, peace, and joy in the Holy Ghost.

You have overcome by the blood of the Lamb and the word of your testimony.

("And they overcame him by the blood of the lamb and by the word of their testimony, and they did not love their lives to the death.") Revelation 12:11.

# September 24

Thank you, Father, for your blood, your glory, and your presence.

I will not withhold anything from them that walks uprightly. ("No good thing will he withhold from those who walk uprightly.") Psalms 84:11. "Mercy triumphs over judgment." James 2:13.

Watchtower. My peace, my justice, my righteousness, my mercy shall overcome evil with good. "Depart from evil and do good; seek peace and pursue it." Psalms 34:14.

# September 25

A daily praise offering and in constant communion with you. Thank you for your goodness and all your blessings. They surround me and overtake me. Your mercy endures forever. "Great is your faithfulness, Lord, unto me." {Thomas Obediah Chisholm}. I walk in your light and gladness. Your mercy triumphs over judgment. Light shines in darkness. Overcome evil with good. Righteous acts of the saints.

Much peace, much joy, much prosperity, much abundance. Richness of the Lord and much joy in the Holy Ghost. You are "A very present help in time of trouble." Psalms 46:1. You are all I need.

## SEPTEMBER 26

This is your special day, Lord: the Day of Atonement. Righteous Judge, thank you for meeting with me and for never leaving me.

Healing is thy portion; deliverance is thy portion.

Meribah: (contemplation).

## SEPTEMBER 27

Thank you, Father that you sup with me. I desire to be in your presence. Forgive all my sins and wash me whiter than snow. A heart of thanksgiving and praise is what my heart is for you.

Thank you for filling me with your joy and gladness. "Do not be overcome by evil, but overcome evil with good." Romans 12:21.

"Mercy triumphs over judgment." James 2:13. "For you shall go out with joy, and be led out with peace." Isaiah 55:11. Thank you for my peaceable habitation and secure dwellings. Thank you for the joy of the Lord, which is my strength, and for quiet resting places. "The fear of the Lord is the beginning of wisdom." Psalms 111:10.

Meribah is another name for Kadesh Barnea. (*Kedesh* means sacred place.) Go in peace.

*Linda Walker*

# SEPTEMBER 28

The set time to favor me has come! Thank you, Lord, for your favor in my life. Thank you for abundance of joy and abundance of peace. "Great peace have those who love my law, and nothing shall cause them to stumble." Psalms 119:165. The ministry of joy and the purpose of joy.

Thank you for the overflowing joy and goodness in my life. Life becomes you.

Life-changing favor and life-changing peace. The fullness of the Lord becomes you.

"Spring up, o well, and make me whole. Spring up, o well, and give to me life abundantly." {L. Casebolt}.

Matchless name. Great grace is upon us all. Rocky Mountain high. Abundant mercy.

*Washington Post.* "Mercy triumphs over judgment." James 2:13. Thank you for the overflowing joy in my life.

"Surely goodness and mercy shall follow me all the days of my life; and I will dwell in the house of the Lord forever." Psalms 23:6.

"Thy kingdom, come thy will be done, on earth as it is in heaven." Matthew 6:10.

Ministry of peace. All is well with my soul. Go in peace and the joy of the Lord.

# OCTOBER

# OCTOBER 03

March to the beat of the drum. Much-needed rest.

You are the great I Am. You are my peace, my healer, my deliverer, my provider, my help, and my guide. "Mercy triumphs over judgment." James 2:13.

Manifested presence of God. The lion and the lamb. "You are a very present help in time of trouble," my very present help in time of need. Psalms 46:1. Breakthrough.

Much faithfulness, much abundance, and much prosperity. Time of grace and atonement.

"Wonderful counselor, mighty God, everlasting Father, Prince of Peace." Isaiah 9:6. King of Kings, Lord of Lords.

I worship you for who you are

# OCTOBER 04

Thank you, Lord, for your Holy Spirit, who helps us in every decision, protects us, and guides us. Help us always to listen and follow the leading of the Holy Spirit. Your way is perfect. Your will for our lives is to do us only good and to bless us. Help us not to do what we want to do, but always to listen to the still, small voice of the Holy Spirit. Let the peace of God be our guide. If there is no peace, only confusion and question, then that is not your perfect will for us. Help me always to seek you first and not just what seems right in my own mind.

"Bless the Lord, o my soul. Bless his holy name." Psalms 103:1.

"Righteousness exalts a nation." Proverbs 14:34. "Thy kingdom come, thy will be done, on earth as it is in heaven." Matthew 6:10.

Your perfect peace and joy is in heaven, and that is your will for earth.

Right standing with God. "My hope is built on nothing less than Jesus Christ and his righteousness." {Edward Mote}. "Hope deferred makes the heart sick." Proverbs 13:12. Wonderful Counselor, soon-coming King. Light of the World, Prince of Peace you are.

Majesty, bright and morning star. Multiplied by thousands upon thousands. Overwhelming love and joy unspeakable and full of your glory. Bread of heaven. *Mitzpah.*

Fill me with your presence. Your words bring new life. Sup with me, Holy Spirit. "The joy of the Lord is my strength," (Nehemiah 8:10) and the Word of the Lord brings life. Life everlasting.

Multiplied by thousands upon thousands   Grandeur. All is well.

I roll my works upon you, Lord, for you care for me. In good times and in bad times, you take care of me. You want only the best for us, to do us good. "Commit your works to the Lord, and your thoughts will be established." Proverbs 16:3.

# OCTOBER 05

For grace and peace by with you in Jesus' name.

Thank you for your precious anointing, Lord. You cover and protect me. Thank you for my husband's anointing that covers me like a veil and protects me from all harm.

Quicken me to never touch whom you have anointed and to do them no harm in any way. We all serve you, Lord, and are ministers of the Lord.

"Though the fig tree may not blossom, nor fruit be on the vines; though the labor of the olive may fail, and the fields yield no food; though the flock may be cut off from the fold, and there be no herd in the stalls, yet I will rejoice in the Lord, I will joy in the God of my salvation. The Lord God is my strength; He will make my feet like deer's feet, and He will make me walk on my high hills" (Habakkuk 3:17–19).

"Bless the Lord, o my soul. Bless his holy name." Psalms 103:1. My joy comes from the Lord, which is my strength.

"Great peace have those who love thy law, and nothing shall cause them to stumble." Psalms 119:165. Matchless name, the great I Am. I Am all that you ever need. You meet every need that I have. Thank you, Father, that every need is met in my life. You make a way for us and bless the work of our hands. Thank you, Lord, that you give me favor.

# OCTOBER 06

Thank you, Father, that you are a rewarder of them that diligently seek you. Seek first the kingdom of God and His righteousness, and all these things shall be added unto you. You make a way where there seems no way. Thank you for the abundance of peace that you give to me.

Righteousness, right standing with God, exalts a nation. "Mercy triumphs over judgment." James 2:13. "No good thing will he withhold from them that walk uprightly." Psalms 84:11. Thank you that you give me the desires of my heart. All is well.

I will repay. Manifested presence of God, matchless name. Everlasting Father, Prince of Peace.

Bless my husband, Lord, for all the sacrifices he has made for so many years and for all he has given to me and this family. Multiply blessings upon blessings upon him. I praise you and thank you for giving him to me.

Trust me. My life is in your hands.

# OCTOBER 08

Thank you, Lord, for the cleansing rain last night, watering everything and causing growth. Thank you for teaching me all about the tabernacle, what everything stands for and the meaning of it all. Give me complete understanding of all your important feasts. Help me know how much you love us as your children and how much you want to bless us with only good always. "Blessings chase the righteous and overtake us." Deuteronomy 28:2. Window of opportunity.

Multitude upon multitude. Everlasting Father, Prince of Peace.

In the tabernacle, in the most holy place, the lampstand provided the light, but in the Holy of Holies your glory was its light.

You are the Light of the World. Lead Lord, by your glory. You are my light and my song.

Have mercy on me and forgive my transgressions and lead me in the way of everlasting.

Teach me your law. "For by you I can run against a troop, and by my God I leap over a wall." Psalms 18:29. "You are a very present help in time of trouble," (Psalms 46:1) my very present help in time of need. All your billows wash over me with your love. Come, my love; come away with me to a place called love.

Magnificent Savior, at the tabernacle of praise leave all your worries and cares behind you.

Come away with me, my love, to a place called "there."

"In your presence is fullness of joy; and at your right hand are pleasures forevermore." Psalms 16:11. All is well.

"Come, Holy Spirit, sweet heavenly dove. Stay right here with us, filling us with your love.

And for these blessings, I lift my voice and say, without a doubt, we know that we have been revived when we leave this place." {Doris Mae Akers}.

# OCTOBER 09

Thank you for your goodness and mercy that go before me and follow me all the days of my life.

Make me a blessing to all whom you send me to, Father. May they see you in me. I represent you. Help me to be excellent in all my ways, Master and Savior, Light of the World, Prince of Peace, everlasting Father, Majesty, and soon-coming King. I walk by faith and not by sight. Mercy Mountain Boys.

"Thy kingdom come, thy will be done, on earth as it is in heaven." Matthew 6:10. "Seek peace and pursue it."

"…Let not your heart be troubled; neither let it be afraid." John 14:27. Shouts of joy.

You are my cloud by day and my fire by night. Holy are you, Lord, and greatly to be praised, who leads me and guides me into all truth. Thank you for opening up the windows of heaven and pouring out such a blessing, we don't have room enough to contain it.

# October 10

Take full control of my life, Lord, and remove what is not like you. Make me a vessel fit for your use. May others see you in me. Help me to encourage them, and help them to draw near to you.

Much peace, much gladness, much righteousness, much genuineness, much expectation, and much boldness. Mountain-moving faith. "Now faith is the substance of things hoped for, the evidence of things not seen." Hebrews 11:1. Righteous Judge.

I apply your spotless blood to this nation. I ask that you forgive us for all the sins of this nation. Wash clean and purify this nation, Lord. I repent for all of the sins of this nation. Give us a brand-new beginning. Help us to do what is pleasing in your sight and to fear you, Lord. Grace be upon us all. Deliver us from all unrighteousness. "Open the windows of heaven pour us out such a blessing that there will not be room enough to receive it all." Malachi 3:10."Deep calls unto deep at the noise of the waterfalls; all your waves and billows have gone over me." Psalms 42:7. Wash over me with your love.

Divine intervention. A city set on a hill, "for he waited for the city which has foundations whose builder and maker is God." Hebrews 11:10. Shower your love upon us. Shower us with your love, o Lord. Destroy the yokes and remove the burdens in people's lives. In Jesus' name. Amen.

Onward, Christian soldier.

# OCTOBER 15

Even in my times of being rejected and hurt, of evil being returned for good, I know that there is nothing that you allow in my life that you will not use to bring something good. Forgive me for the times I was not walking closer to you and did not acknowledge your love. Now I understand your broken heart of rejection. Forgive me, Lord.

Help me to love and forgive others. To know the love of God that surpasses all understanding.

Thank you for the breakthrough. Bondservants.

"His eye is on the sparrow, and I know he watches me." {Civilla D. Martin}.

Much healing, much restoration, and much holiness.

"And we know that all things work together for good to those who love God, to those who are the called according to his purpose." Romans 8:28.

In the good times and the bad times.

"And all these blessings shall come upon you and overtake you." Deuteronomy 28:2. Much prosperity and much abundance.

Thank you for your abundance of mercy.

I will call upon the Lord while he is near. ("Seek the Lord while he may be found call upon him while he is near.") Isaiah 55:6. Abundance of grace and overflowing love.

"Mercy triumphs over judgment" (James 2:13). In my place of abundance. Overflowing joy in our lives.

*Linda Walker*

The best of the best. We are to enjoy our lives to the fullest. Overflowing love.

This is a time of great peace and a time of rich blessings. Your words to me are more precious than silver or gold.

## OCTOBER 16

Thank you, Lord that you are with me each step of the way on this journey. Thank you for giving me times of refreshment and rest and blessing along the way. Give me understanding of what you spoke to me this morning, "a place called 'there.'"

"And you will seek me and find me, when you search for me with all your heart." Jeremiah 29:13. A life filled with your glory and passion is what I seek. Thank you for the abundance of peace, loving kindness, mercy, grace, rich fulfillment, and overflowing love. Everlasting Father, Prince of Peace, thank you for the joy of the Lord, which is my strength. "My help comes from the Lord, who made heaven and earth." Psalms 121:2.

Come, my beloved; come away with me to a place called "there."

March onward.

## OCTOBER 17

"Blessed is the nation whose God is the Lord." Psalms 33:12. "Make known his deeds among the people." Psalms 105:1. The righteous acts of the saints. "Mercy triumphs over judgment." James 2:13. "The fear of the Lord is the beginning of wisdom." Psalms 111:10. Bright lights. The sovereignty of the Lord, our righteous Judge.

Atonement.

Widespread famine.

…"The wealth of the sinner is stored up for the righteous." Proverbs 13:22. "They that seek the Lord shall not lack any good thing." Psalms 34:10.

Stock market collapse.

"Some trust in chariots, and some trust in horses; but we will remember the name of the lord our God." Psalms 20:7. My hope is in the Lord. "My hope is built on nothing less than Jesus' blood and righteousness." {Edward Mote}.

"But those that wait on the Lord shall renew their strength; they shall mount up with wings like eagles, they shall run and not grow weary, they shall walk and not faint." Isaiah 40:31.

# OCTOBER 18

Thank you, Father, for the compassion that you have toward us. "Because His compassions fail not they are new every morning; great is your faithfulness." Lamentations 3:22-23. Thank you for giving us your compassion and providing a way of escape for us. Great is thy faithfulness.

Thank you for teaching us to give so that you will multiply it back to us, pressed down, shaken together, and running over. ("Give and it will be given to you: good measure, pressed down, shaken together, and running over will be put into your bosom. For with the same measure that you use, it will be measured back to you.") Luke 6:38. Great acts of the saints.

Contagious faith.

"Many are the afflictions of the righteous, but the Lord delivers him out of them all." Psalms 34:19. Cornfield.

"Blessed is the nation whose God is the Lord." Psalms 33:12.

"From the rising of the sun to its going down the Lord's name is to be praised." Psalms 113:3.

Thank you for your provision and meeting our needs daily. Thank you for your protection. Thank you for the Holy Spirit guiding us each day. Your name is greatly to be praised.

My provider, my protector, my healer, my deliverer, my soon-coming King, my Master, my Savior, and my high tower.

We make our requests known to you and you take our requests to the Father. ("Be anxious for nothing, but in everything by prayer and supplication, with thanksgiving, let your requests be made known to God.") Philippians 4:6. We have whatsoever we ask of you because you go to the Father. We believe that we receive. The prayers of the saints, multiplied by thousands upon thousands as you go before us, making the crooked places straight and the rough places smooth.

"Your mercies are new every morning. Great is your faithfulness." Lamentations 3:22.

Much joy, much happiness, much peace, much provision, and much abundance.

"Not by might nor by power, but by my spirit, saith the Lord." Zechariah 4:6.

Bengazi. Protect our military in Bengazi.

"Rock of ages, cleft for me, let me hide myself in thee." {Augustus Montague Toplady}. Thank you that you are right beside me.

Hopeful. "Mercy triumphs over judgment." James 2:13.

"But the wealth of the sinner is stored up for the righteous." Proverbs 13:22.

Miami-Dade.

"How great thou art, how great thou art." {Stuart K. Hine}.

Whispering pines.

"Your rod and your staff, they comfort me. You prepare a table before me in the presence of my enemies; you anoint my head with oil; my cup runs over. Surely goodness and mercy shall follow me all the days of my life; and I will dwell in the house of the Lord forever." Psalms 23:4-6.

You encompass about me as with a shield; my cup runneth over.

The angels of the Lord encamp about me, causing me to triumph over my enemies.

Thank you for delivering me from every bondage and sin.

The yoke-destroying, burden-removing power of God. Reveal your glory through me.

Your anointing is working through me and in me, causing me to have abundance of peace and joy in the Holy Ghost. Creator and Maker of heaven and earth, holy are you, Lord. How great thou art, how great thou art.

Majesty on high. Much anointing, much power, much peace, much longevity, much abundance, and the joy of the Lord, which is my strength.

*Washington Post.*

Much faithfulness, much holiness, much remembrance of you, my King.

Faithful one, endeavor to do my will. Riches and honor await you.

# October 22

Houses and riches belong to you. My cup runneth over. Your mercy and goodness chase me and overtake me.

"Righteousness exalts a nation." Proverbs 14:34.

Holy are you, Lord. In God we trust. Surround us with songs of deliverance. I speak healing over this nation. Healing for the nation of the Lord. Righteousness cries out to God.

Peace be still. Peace be unto all nations. In Jesus' name.

Righteous acts of the saints. Blessed be the name of the Lord.

"Thy kingdom come, thy will be done, on earth as it is in heaven." Matthew 6:10.

Meet with me in the sanctuary.

"But above all these things put on love, which is the bond of perfection." Colossians 3:14. Comfort me with the comfort which comes only from you my glory and my King, My soon-coming King to take his bride away. Marsh.

Much abundance of peace shall fill your heart. Cry out to me, o righteous one, and I will give you peace.

National disaster.

Abundance of prosperity, abundance of joy, and abundance of peace. "The fear of the Lord is the beginning of wisdom." Psalms 111:10.

You shall have peace from all sides in your sanctuary of love.

# OCTOBER 24

Permit me to make you well with the healing touch of the Lord.

Messages from heaven. Much happiness, much joy, much peace, much prosperity, and much love. Abundance of goodness, faithfulness, and the presence of God. Much forgiveness and joy in the Holy Ghost. "Whispering Pines."

My abundance flows, a source of ministry. *Mekadesh.* (The Lord who sanctifies.)

Abundant supply and rich resources.

# OCTOBER 25

Thank you, Lord, for your mercy and forgiveness. Help me to extend mercy and forgiveness to others. Thank you that mercy triumphs over judgment. As we judge and show mercy to others, that is how you will judge and show mercy toward us. "Righteousness exalts a nation." Proverbs 14:34.

"Thy kingdom come, thy will be done, on earth as it is in heaven" Matthew 6:10—which is righteousness, peace, and joy in the Holy Spirit.

"However when he, the Spirit of truth has come, he will guide you into all truth." John 16:13. "Forsake not yourselves from assembling together." Hebrews 10:25. Richness and the favor of God. "Not by might nor by power, but by my Spirit, saith the Lord of hosts" (Zechariah 4:6) who made heaven and earth. Trust not in riches and seek not the things of this world. "Seek first the kingdom of God and His righteousness, and all these things shall be added unto you." Matthew 6:33. Seek not the things of this world nor trust in riches, for "I am the way, the truth, and the life. For no one comes to the Father except through me." (Jesus Christ.) John 14:6.

Wisdom, righteousness, sanctification, redemption, and the fear of the Lord in abundant supply. Transcript.

Wash over me with your love. Total peace and total joy belong to me with joy unspeakable and full of your glory. "Whispering Pines." Share the joy, my love.

"Blessed assurance Jesus is mine"{Fanny J. Crosby}. Matchless name above all else.

Rock-solid faith.

# OCTOBER 28

Thank you, Lord, for speaking to me in my dreams and visions and also speaking to my spirit. Thank you for miracles coming and for instructing me concerning the book. Bless your people, Lord, with your Word, so that we have wisdom and direction for our lives.

Make every effort to walk in my ways. Thank you for setting me free from the spirit of fear: fear of failure, fear of man's approval, and fear of acceptance. "Therefore if the Son makes you free, you shall be free indeed." John 8:36. "Now the Lord is the Spirit; where the Spirit of the Lord is, there is liberty." 2 Corinthians 3:17.

I bask in your love. Multiplied by hundreds of thousands.

The river of love, the love that is shed abroad in our hearts by the Holy Spirit.

Thank you for the Holy Spirit, our help, our comforter, our teacher, our guide, giving us power to carry out all you've called us to do.

I live to please you, Lord.

Conservative view.

In all things, give me praise. With all that is within me, I give you praise.

Mkaddish (The Lord who sanctifies).

A place of freedom from all fears in in your presence—a place called "there." "And you will seek me and find me, when you search for me with all your heart." Jeremiah 29:13. One night with the King.

Blessed Redeemer, Prince of Peace, Almighty God.

Magical moments. Let all the earth rejoice, for "great is the Lord and greatly to be praised." Psalms 48:1. Maker of heaven and earth, my soon-coming King.

"Blessed is the nation whose God is the Lord." Psalms 33:12.

"In all thy ways acknowledge him, and he will direct your paths" (Proverbs 3:6) and make your paths straight.

"The wealth of the wicked (sinner) is stored up for the righteous." Proverbs 13:22. Multiplied by thousands upon thousands.

Bedrock of faith, overcoming power of God. March madness.

Much joy, much peace, much prosperity, much abundance, much grace, much love, much ability, much determination, and much forgiveness.

All-knowing and all-powerful God. Much grace and anointing and the abundance of peace in your presence.

# OCTOBER 30

Prisoner of hope, hope thou in me. ("Return to the stronghold, you prisoners of hope. Even today I declare that I will restore double to you." Zechariah 9:12. "Why are you cast down, O my soul? And why are you disquieted within me? Hope in God; for I shall yet praise Him, the help of my countenance and my God.") Psalms 42:11.

# OCTOBER 31

Prince of Peace, our righteous Judge.

I clearly hear the voice of the Holy Spirit revealing your heart of love to the Father.

Much peace, much joy, much love. "Therefore do not cast away your confidence, which has great reward." Hebrews 10:35. Your blessings overtake us. Blessings are forthcoming. Money cometh.

Praise to my King. March forward with revelation, knowledge, and the fear of the Lord.

Light up my life with your revelation. Much joy and happiness, much peace and prosperity, my love, my love, my love.

Wisdom, righteousness, sanctification, and redemption. ("But of him you are in Christ Jesus, who became for us wisdom from God and righteousness and sanctification and redemption".) 1 Corinthians 1:30. "The leading edge." (Magazine article.)

Grace be upon you.

.

# NOVEMBER

# November 01

Thank you, Lord, for your yoke-destroying and burden-removing power in my life.

You're my ever-present help in time of need. ("God is our refuge and strength, a very present help in trouble.") I will speak truth, and the truth shall make me free.

Apopka.

Covenant of peace and prosperity, abundance and the fear of the Lord.

Help me, Holy Spirit, to stay focused on what you've called me to do.

Watchful eye. "Leading edge." (Magazine article).

"My hope is built on nothing less than Jesus' blood and righteousness." {Edward Mote}.

Hasten to do my will. Money cometh.

I speak love, joy, and peace in all of its abundance into this home. In Jesus' name. I make a way where there seems no way and overcome darkness with light. Much abundance where there has been sorrow. I give joy, abundant life to the fullness overflowing, and full of my glory.

March madness.

"But Above all these things put on love, which is the bond of perfection." Colossians 3:14. "Love endures long and is patient and kind; Love never is envious nor boils over with jealousy, Love is not boastful or vainglorious, does not display it self haughtily. It is not conceited; it is not rude (unmannerly) and does not act unbecomingly. Love (Gods love in us) does not insist on its own

*Linda Walker*

rights or its own way, for it is not self-seeking; it is not touchy or fretful or resentful; it takes not account of the evil done to it (pays no attention to a suffered wrong). Love rejoices when right and truth prevail. Love bears up under anything and everything that comes is ready to believe the best of every person, its hopes are fadeless under all circumstances, and it endures everything without weakening. Love never fails." 1 Corinthians 13:4-8 (Amplified Version.) Love always is concerned about the welfare of others. Love thinks no evil, bears no evil, sees no evil.

Live on purpose. Live life to the fullest.

# November 02

Help me to become more like you every day, Lord. Help me, Holy Spirit, to be more aware of the spiritual realm than the natural realm. May I walk in the Spirit, produce the fruit of the Spirit, and worship you always. For without me you can do nothing, but with me all things are possible. "Blessed are the righteous and their seed shall be mighty upon the earth. Wealth and riches shall be in their house." Psalms 112:1-3. Nuggets of gold. Bright and morning star.

Much proficiency, much boldness, and much consistency.

River of life. Rivers of living water fill my heart. Appointed and anointed, in God we trust.

"Trust in the Lord with all your heart and lean not on your own understanding; in all your ways acknowledge him, and he shall direct your paths." Proverbs 3:5-6. Positive change.

Much wealth, much riches, and much prosperity. Above all else, acknowledge him and he shall direct your path. (Think big.)

"Many are the afflictions of the righteous, but the Lord delivers him out of them all." Psalms 34:19.

Righteous acts of the saints. Meditate on my Word. My Word gives light and life.

Be obedient to all my word. "Then you shall make your way prosperous; then you shall have good success." Reach out and touch someone today. Be my hands and heart extended. Weary warriors. (This book of the law shall not depart from your mouth, but you shall meditate in it day and night, that you may observe to do according to all that is written in it. For then you will make your way prosperous, and then you will have good success). Joshua 1:8.

Gateway to heaven. Everywhere I go, a positive change will occur. Abundance of peace and prosperity shall be mine. In Jesus' name. Wealth and riches shall be in my house and the fear of the Lord.

# November 05

"Rock of ages, cleft for me, let me hide myself in thee." {Augustus Montague Toplady}.

"Come unto me, all you who labor and are heavy laden, and I will give you rest." Matthew 11:28.

Speak to me, Holy Spirit, and give me direction and wisdom and knowledge. Help me today to know exactly what you would have me say, so that it may give life and peace to all who hear it. Thank you for wisdom from above and for the ministry of reconciliation. Onward, Christian soldier.

Be reconciled to the Lord, the lover of your soul. "In your presence is fullness of joy; and at your right hand are pleasures forevermore." Psalms 16:11.

Much happiness, much joy, much love, much peace, much abundance, much prosperity. "Seek peace and pursue it." Psalms 34:14. "Peace I leave with you, my peace I give unto you; not as the world gives do I give to you. Let not your hearts be troubled, neither let them be afraid." John 14:27.

# November 06

You hide me in the cleft of the rock. Consecrate unto me.

Westminster Abbey.

Divine secrets from the Lord, "Prince of Peace, everlasting Father, Emmanuel, God with us." Isaiah 9:6.

Out of my belly will flow rivers of living water. ("He who believes in me, as the scripture has said, out of his heart will flow rivers of living water.") John 7:38.

Watch and pray. Revelation, wisdom, and knowledge. March madness.

"From the rising of the sun to it's the going down the Lord's name is to be praised." Psalms 113:3.

Belfast, Ireland.

Manifested presence of God.

Much, much peace and prosperity.

# November 07

Breakthrough   Thank you, Lord, for the breakthrough. Step out and do not be afraid. I will be with you to help you and comfort you. Make no mistake: I am with you and will never leave you nor forsake you. Great is my faithfulness. "Many are the afflictions of the righteous, but I will deliver them out of them all." Psalms 34:19. "Thy kingdom come, thy will be done, on earth as it is in heaven." Matthew 6:10.

Much greatness and sovereignty. "One nation, under God, indivisible, with liberty and justice for all."

Abundance of peace and prosperity. "Surely goodness and mercy shall follow me all the days of my life." Psalms 23:6.

"With long life you will satisfy us and show us thy salvation. Psalms 91:16. Much fulfillment.

"Mercy triumphs over judgment." James 2:13.

Exceptional praise and great grace was upon them all.

Thank you for "goodness and mercy following me all the days of my life." Psalms 23:6.

Rivers of living water, abundance of mercy, and peace. Matchless love.

"Come unto me, all you who labor and are heavy laden, and I will give you rest." "Do not cast me away from your presence, and do not take thy Holy Spirit from me. Restore unto me the joy of thy salvation, and uphold me by your generous Spirit." Matthew 11:28. For is there not a cause?

Mighty acts of the saints. Reveal your heart of love to me, Lord.

# November 09

Manifest your presence in my life today, Lord. "Great peace have those who love thy law, and nothing shall cause them to stumble." Psalms 119:165. Keep me and hide me in your Word, Lord, so that peace floods my soul and overwhelms me with your joy.

Righteous one, manifested presence of the Lord. March madness.

"Lengthen your cords and strengthen your stakes," (Isaiah 54:2) for the Lord your God goes with you wherever you go. You are never alone. Pour out your Spirit upon all flesh. Your sons and daughters shall prophesy, your old men shall dream dreams, and your young men shall have visions. I will pour out my Spirit in these last days upon all flesh. ("And it shall come to pass afterward that I will pour out my Spirit on all flesh; your sons and your daughters shall prophesy, your old men shall dream dreams, your young men shall see visions. And also on my menservants and on my maidservants I will pour out my Spirit in those days.") Acts 2:17-18.

# November 10

Thank you for your Word, Lord. Thank you for all the promises in your Word, which is my weapon of warfare, which is mighty to the pulling down of strongholds. Thank you that you promise us that we are never alone; you always go with us.

"I will lift up my eyes to the hill from whence comes my help? My help comes from the Lord who made Heaven and earth." Psalms 121:1-2. "The Lord shall preserve you from all evil; he shall preserve your soul. The Lord shall preserve you're going out and you're coming in from this time forth and even forevermore." Ps. 121:7-8.

Thank you, Lord, that you protect me from all evil. You go with me everywhere I go. Thank you for letting me know that the message titles you spoke to me are for the magazine. I will get busy and work on them. You will accomplish much.

Mountain-moving faith. (Sizable ad.)

Mercy ministries. "My help comes from the Lord." Psalms 121:2.

(Watchtower).

"A place called there." (A message for magazine).

My peace I give unto you, many blessings. Bask in my love, joyful one, joyful one.

Thank you for the daily strength to overcome the Evil One.

*Miami Herald.*

"Not by might nor by power, but by my Spirit, saith the Lord." Zechariah 4:6.

# November 12

Spirit, soul, and body.

March madness.

Peace be within our walls. Fill me to overflowing with your presence. Peace be within our borders. ("For he has strengthened the bars of your gates; he has blessed your children within you. He makes peace in your borders, and fills you with the finest wheat.") Psalms 147:13-14. Righteous nation. "I will lift up my eyes to the hills from whence comes my help. My help comes from the Lord, the maker of heaven and earth." Psalms 121:1-2.

Fresh revelation from the Lord. Merciful Savior.

Righteous one, much joy and fulfillment. "The blessing of the Lord it makes rich and he adds no sorrow with it." Proverbs 10:22. Whispering pines.

# November 13

Much happiness and much love.

Rivers of living water. "Eye has not seen, nor ear heard, nor have entered into the heart of man the things which God has prepared for those who love him" 1 Corinthians 2:9 " who are the called according to my purposes." Romans 8:28.

"Great peace have those who love thy law and nothing shall cause them to be offended." Psalms 119:165.

Magnificent Savior, Prince of Peace, mighty God, everlasting Father.

"Come unto me, all you who labor and are and heavy laden, and I will give you rest."

"Take my yoke upon you and learn from me, for I am gentle and lowly in heart, and you will find rest for your souls. For my yoke is easy and my burden is light." Matthew 11:28-30.

Come away with me, my beloved, and I will give you rest. My God and my Lord. Master, Savior, Prince of Peace, mighty God.

# November 14

You are a mighty God, "but you, O Lord are a shield for me, my glory, and the one who lifts up my head" Psalms 3:3 and lover of my soul.

Thank you that I am built upon the solid foundation, the solid Rock of you, Lord. Thank you that you are always with me. "Your rod and your staff, they comfort me you prepare a table before me in the presence of my enemies. Surely goodness and mercy shall follow me all the days of my life, and I will dwell in the house of the Lord forever." Psalms 23:4-6.

Miracles, signs, and wonders belong to me. My life is built on nothing less than Jesus' love and righteousness. Thank you for wisdom from above much happiness, much love, and much joy and peace filling my heart to overflowing in the presence of the Lord. Majesty on high.

Abundance.

Rivers of living water and richness of the Lord.

"By your stripes I am healed." Thank you, for you surround me and keep me safe from all around. ("Who Himself bore our sins in His own body on the tree, that we, having died to sins, might live for righteousness-by whose stripes you were healed.") 1 Peter 2:24.

Share your testimony.

Thank you that the anointing destroys every yoke and removes every burden in people's lives.

"O Magnify the Lord with me and let us exalt His name together." Psalms 34:3. My all-consuming one.

High upon the rock, I will hide you in the cleft. "The prayers of the saints availeth much". James 5:16.

Much love and freedom.

# November 15

Thank you, Father, for helping me share what you put in my heart to share at the first speaking engagement about my book. I pray that they will desire to seek you more intimately and draw closer to you. Thank you that my husband came to support me. Minister to my husband today, Lord, and bless everything that he does. Forgive me for all of my sins, Lord.

McIntosh.

"Many are the afflictions of the righteous, but you deliver them out of them all." Psalms 34:19. Minister of the gospel, minister of righteousness. Captivate my heart, o Lord. "The blessing of the Lord maketh rich and He addeth no sorrow with it." Proverbs 10:22. Come forth, my love, to our place of prayer.

The voice of many waters.

Much love, much peace, much joy, much happiness, much abundance much prosperity, and the fear of the Lord. Roll your works upon me, for I care for you and I will not leave you or forsake you.

"Seek first the kingdom of God and His righteousness, and all these things shall be added unto you." Matthew 6:33.

McIntosh.

Much joy, much rejoicing, much embracing, much favor, much fulfillment, and much blessings.

Divine order and prosperity bring about change. Much wisdom forever settled in heaven.

# November 16

Thank you, Father, for all the book signings that I have done. Bless all who have welcomed me so warmly. Be with me tonight as I do the first book signing here in my hometown.

Bless Brenda's business. May many come and be blessed by your presence. May the book, *My Journey*, minister and bless all who read it. Thank you for all you are doing in my life right now. Thank you for bringing former friends into my life to bless and encourage me. Thank you for totally restoring all. You are my sun and shield, and nothing shall by any means harm me. Restoration.

"And they overcame him by the blood of the lamb and by the word of their testimony, and they did not love their lives to the death." Revelation 12:11. You have overcome by the blood of the Lamb and the word of my testimony.

Service to the Lord upon my request. Your billows wash over me with love.

Many accomplishments. Run, river, run. Fill my heart to overflowing, basking in your love and presence.

In you I live and breathe and have my being. ("For in Him we live and move and have our being.") Acts 17:28. Much accomplishment.

Direct my steps and make them sure. "Who satisfies my mouth with good things, so that my youth is renewed like the eagles." Psalms 103:5. "O magnify the Lord with me, and let us exalt His name together." Psalms 34:3.

Make me a vessel fit for your use, amongst many brethren.

"Apple of my eye." Zechariah 2:8. Songs of deliverance.

March on.

# NOVEMBER 19

"Blessed is the man that feareth the Lord, who delights greatly in his commandments. His seed shall be mighty upon the earth. Wealth and riches shall be in his house, and his righteousness endures forever." Psalms 112:1-3.

Thank you, Lord, for wisdom from above and the fear of the Lord, which is my strength.

Wisdom, righteousness, sanctification, and redemption belong to me. "Now the just shall live by faith." Hebrews 10:38. Thank you for your blood that makes me whole again. "O precious is that flow that makes me white as snow no other fount I know, nothing but the blood of Jesus." {Robert Lowry}. By your stripes I am made whole.

"Blessings chase us and overtake us." Deuteronomy 28:2.

March on.

# NOVEMBER 20

What you have blessed, the enemy cannot curse. Thank you, Father, for healing and deliverance that belong to me and all who believe in you.

Thank you for bringing our son and our grandchildren over yesterday. What a blessing. Thank you for the restoration you've promised to us. Minister healing today to this family, Lord, I ask. "Mercy triumphs over judgment." James 2:13. Righteous acts of the saints.

Much happiness, much love, much peace, and much adoration. My Savior, my King of everything.

Masterpiece. Enjoying everyday life to the full.

Righteous Judge.

"The blessing of the Lord makes us rich, and you add no sorrow with it." Proverbs 10:22. McIntosh.

# November 21

"Hope thou in me." Psalms 42:11. Blessings upon blessings belong to you.

Righteous Judge. I welcome you, Holy Spirit. For all your love, Lord, I thank you. For all your peace, I thank you. For all your joy, Lord, I thank you. For all your care, Lord, I thank you.

March forward.

"For I will contend with him who contends with you, and I will save thy children." Isaiah 49:25.

Onward, Christian soldier.

March madness. Agape love. Fill my heart with gladness, and help me be a blessing to many.

Hurricane Sandy (trick of the enemy). Righteous judge.

# November 26

Thank you, Father, that "whom the Son sets free is free indeed." John 8:36. Free to do as you ask me to do.

Riches and honor, wisdom and righteousness, and the fear of the Lord belong to me.

All praise and honor belong to you, Lord. Worship the King in all his majesty. McIntosh.

Soon-coming King.

# November 27

March madness.

Thank you that you are my King of Kings and Lord of Lords. Thank you that you are my healer, my deliverer, my provider, my Prince of Peace, my mighty God, Master of all.

You work all things together for our good, my helper and my comforter. Your mercy endureth forever. I trust you, for you work all things together for our good.

"Your word is a lamp unto my feet and a light unto my path." Psalm 119:105. "Your righteousness endures forever. Wealth and riches shall be in our house." Psalms 112:3. "Blessed assurance, Jesus is mine." {Fanny J. Crosby}. You are my life, my strength, my ever-present help in time of need. ("God is our refuge and strength, a very present help in trouble.") Psalms 46:1. Merciful Savior, Prince of Peace, everlasting Father, mighty God. "Blessed assurance, Jesus is mine." I have all power and authority over the Evil One, and nothing shall by any means harm me. "Your rod and your staff, they comfort me," and my righteousness endures forever. ("Behold, I give you the authority to trample on serpents and scorpions, and over all the power of the enemy, and nothing shall by any means hurt you.") Luke 10:19.

# NOVEMBER 28

I shall walk in your supernatural strength and look to you for my direction, for my hope, for the answer to all of my concerns.

Thank you for the good plan that you have for me and mine, to prosper us and not to harm us, and to give us a future and a hope. Settle disputes. "Mercy triumphs over judgment." James 2:13.

("For I know the thoughts that I think toward you, says the Lord, thoughts of peace and not of evil, to give you a future and a hope.") Jeremiah 29:11.

Fulfill your call. "Bond of perfectness." (Title of magazine article.)

River of love, wash over me with your love, your peace, and your joy.

Much holiness, much happiness, much love, much joy, much praise, much abundance.

Corporate ladder. Wisdom from above. March madness. McIntosh.

Fresh and anew. Rejuvenating.

# November 30

Thank you, Father, that it is you and only you who knows my every move. Thank you for teaching me your Word to perfect me. As "I wait upon the Lord, you renew my strength. I shall mount up with wings as eagles, I shall run and not be weary, I shall walk and not faint." Isaiah 40:31. "My help comes from the Lord, the maker of heaven and earth." Psalms 121:1.

"You will perfect that which concerns me," Psalms 138:8 and you make all things brand new. Thank you that it is a brand-new day and that you are our way maker.

"Many are the afflictions of the righteous, but you deliver them out of them all." Psalms 34:19. "Blessings chase us and overtake us." Deuteronomy 28:2. Honor and majesty belong to you.

Thank you for fulfilling the number of our days. Riches shall be in our house.

"Surely goodness and mercy shall follow me all the days of my life," (Psalms 23:6) riches and honor and the fear of the Lord. Grace and peace be multiplied to you wisdom, righteousness, sanctification, and redemption. Breathe on me, Holy Spirit.

Much faithfulness, much joy, much peace, much prosperity, much endurance, and much vindication. Assemble together. March madness.

Joyful hearts be led by me. I will make your way sure. Come aside and know me. Know my name. Cast all your care upon me.

"Let not your hearts be troubled; neither let them be afraid." John 14:27.

You are working all things together for our good. Trust not in the ways of man. In me and me alone put all your trust. "Hope thou in Me." Psalms 42:11.

"Cast all your bread upon the waters; for you will find it after many days." Ecclesiastes 11:1.

Wonderful Savior, wonder Counselor, Prince of Peace, mighty God, almighty Savior.

You are a work in progress.

Matchless name, righteous King, Master of the universe, soon-coming King, Master of everything.

"Bright and morning star" you are. Righteous Judge. Revelation 22:16.

Cry aloud to me. "I will never leave you or forsake you." Hebrews 13:5.

Wash over me with your love.

Pearl of great price. Blessed be my Lord and Savior. Lord of everything, conqueror of death, hell, and the grave. *Mitzpah.* (Means watchtower.) Endless time for all eternity, Savior of the world.

King of Kings and Lord of Lords. Abundant prosperity. My strong tower and my defense.

# DECEMBER

# December 03

Thank you, Lord, that I am never alone. You are always with me, and I go nowhere that you are not there. You know everything about me. "Search me, o God, and know my heart; try me and know my anxieties; and see if there is any wicked way in me, and lead me in the way of everlasting." Psalms 139:23-24. Fill me to overflowing with your love and peace. Make your ways known unto me, Lord. Daily do I seek you, Lord.

"You are the Light of the World," (Matthew 5:14) Maker of heaven and earth and all that is in it. You make me lie down and my sleep is sweet; ("When you lie down, you will not be afraid; yes, you will lie down and your sleep will be sweet".) Proverbs 3:24 my soul waits for you in a dry and thirsty land. Fill us with your mighty power. Your ways are higher than my ways; your thoughts are higher than my thoughts. ("For my thoughts are not your thoughts, nor are your ways my ways says the Lord.") Isaiah55:8.

Fill my heart with your love and awaken us to hear you, Lord.

March madness.

"Whispering pines."

"For Unto us a child is born, unto us a Son is given, and the government shall be upon his shoulders. And his name will be called wonderful, counselor, mighty God, everlasting father, prince of peace.") Isaiah 9:6.

Much peace, much prosperity, much provision, much abundance, much joy, much love, much fellowship.

"Hope thou in me." Psalms 42:11.

Forever loved.

# December 04

Father, help me to walk in your love at all times. Shine the light of your love upon me always and help me to stay in the path you have prepared for me. Thank you for giving me the books that you have given to me. Lead me in every way concerning them. March madness.

Holy ground.

"Behold the maidservant of the lord. Let it be unto me according to thy word." Luke 1:38. "Righteousness exalts a nation." Proverbs 14:34. Thank you for this place of peace and abundance, prosperity and fulfillment.

Thank you for much peace and much joy, and the rivers of love filling our hearts and overtaking our lives.

# December 05

Holiness unto the Lord. Help me to obey you in all things and to be an example of you, Lord.

Ministry of helps.

Wishing you much prosperity and much peace, wisdom, righteousness, sanctification, and redemption in the Holy Spirit.

Come away with me and be ye separate, saith the Lord.

Fit for the Master's use. King of Kings and Lord of lords.

Soon-coming King.

Riches shall be in our house and great shall be the peace of our children.

# December 06

Thank you, Lord, that you are the lover of my soul. My soul thirsts for you. You are my peace upon this earth. I am forever loved by you in the midst of this perverse and crooked nation. Thank you that I am fearfully and wonderfully made. ("I will praise you, for I am fearfully and wonderfully made; marvelous are your works, and that my soul knows very well.") Psalms 139:14.

Holy Spirit, keep me focused on you day and night, I ask. Come, Holy Spirit; fill me with your love.

March madness.

Thank you for whispering pines. Dearly beloved, rest in peace.

Clothe yourself in my love. Righteousness and moral rectitude, abundance of peace and prosperity. Come, Holy Spirit, and dine with me. Manifest your presence in our lives.

Watchtower.

Sweep over me with your love. Master, Savior, Prince of Peace, mighty God, everlasting Father. Make known your ways to me. Thank you for your mercy and your grace. Thank you for giving me your fulfillment and your love and for blessing me with your excellence.

Endeavor to do your best.

Meet me in the garden.

Thank you for supplying all my needs. Suffice me to do your will.

# DECEMBER 07

Thank you, Father, that you are my covering. You protect me on all sides from evil. It is your will for me that I obey. Not my will but thy will, o Lord. Come let us gather together and partake of my perfect will for your life.

"Blessed are the righteous, and their seed shall be mighty upon this earth. Wealth and riches shall be in their house; their righteousness endures forever." Psalms 112:2-3. "Great peace have those who love thy law, and nothing shall cause them to stumble." Psalms 119:165.

"Not forsaking the assembling of ourselves together, as is the manner of some, but exhorting one another and so much the more as you see the day approaching." Hebrews 10:25.

"Righteousness exalts a nation." Proverbs 14:34. Tried and true.

Wisdom from above.

Much happiness, much peace, much prosperity, and much abundance.

"Have thine own way, Lord, have thine own way." {Adelaide A. Plllard}. Right standing with the Lord.

"Cast your bread upon the water for you will find it after many days." Ecclesiastes:11-1. Righteousness and moral rectitude.

Wisdom from above is what I ask of you. Much money, much happiness, much joy, and much love.

You hide me in the shelter of your arms from the attacks of the Evil One.

Come, Holy Spirit, refresh us with your presence. "Do not lead us into temptation, but deliver us from the evil one. For yours is the kingdom and the power and the glory forever. Amen." Matthew 6:13.

"Thy kingdom come, thy will be done, on earth as it is in heaven." Matthew 6:10. My will for you is peace, prosperity, and abundance.

Occupy until I come. Much to do, many to reach.

Wisdom from above will accompany my peace. Roll all your care upon me, for I care for you. "Many are the afflictions of the righteous, but the Lord will deliver them out of them all." Psalms 34:19.

"Whispering Pines."

For under your feathers I shall take refuge. ("He shall cover you with his feathers, and under his wings you shall take refuge.") Psalms 91:4.

The bridegroom cometh.

Make way for the coming of the Lord. Our God reigns.

"I shall abide under the shadow of the Almighty. Only with my eyes shall I look and see the reward of the wicked; it shall not come nigh you." Psalms 91:1,8,10.

Rest in me, my child. "Call to me and I will answer you, and show you great and mighty things, which you do not know." Jeremiah 33:3. I will be with you in trouble and I will help you. "He shall call upon Me, and I will answer him; I will be with him in trouble; I will deliver him and honor him." Psalms 91:15.

Rest in me. Surely I will be with you.

# December 10

Holy Spirit, help me daily to guard the words of my mouth. Help me to always build up and edify others and never speak in a judgmental way toward anyone.

Love out of a pure heart never condemns anyone. "Mercy triumphs over judgment." James 2:13.

"There is therefore now no condemnation to those who are in Christ Jesus, who do not walk according to the flesh, but walk according to the Spirit." Romans 8:1.

"But those who wait upon the Lord shall renew their strength; they shall mount up with wings as eagles, they shall run and not be weary, they shall walk and not faint." Isaiah 40:31.

Much loveliness.

Wonderful Savior, Prince of Peace, bright and morning star. Stay focused.

"But wisdom that is from above is first pure, then peaceable, gentle, willing to yield, full of mercy and good fruits." James 3:17.

Everlasting Father, Prince of Peace.

Much-needed rest. Lover of my soul.

We dwell in peaceable habitations and quiet resting places. ("My people will dwell in a peaceful habitation, in secure dwellings, and in quiet resting places.")

Much to do, places to go, and places to see.

Prophecy of the Lord coming to pass with a willing heart.

"Thy kingdom come, thy will be done, on earth as it is in heaven." Matthew 6:10.

Global ministry.

O hail, King Jesus.

"O magnify the Lord with me, and let us exalt His name together." Psalms 34:3. Worship the King above all else.

United we stand, divided we fall. Grace and peace be unto you. Blessed be the Lord.

Go forth. Be my hands and feet. ("Go therefore and make disciples of all nations, baptizing them in the name of the Father and the Son and the Holy Spirit." Matthew 28:19.

I am with you always; go and do likewise.

Vision coming to pass. You are on the right path.

I hear the voice of the Holy Spirit, and the voice of a stranger I will not follow.

("Yet they will by no means follow a stranger, but will flee from him, for they do not know the voice of strangers.") John 10:5.

Come, take up your cross and follow me.

Onward, Christian soldier.

# DECEMBER 11

Much grief and much sorrow comes from an unrepentant heart. "Peace I leave with you, my peace I give to you not as the world gives do I give to you.

Let not your hearts be troubled neither let it be afraid." John 14:27.

"Go tell it on the mountain, and over the hills and everywhere. Go tell it on the mountain that Jesus Christ is born." {John Wesley Work Jr.}.

Much joy and happiness comes from me.

My love lasts a lifetime. "For whom the Lord loves, he corrects, just as a father the son in whom he delights." Proverbs 3:12. "Go and sin no more." John 8:11.

The righteous acts of the saints.

"Heal me, o Lord, and I shall be healed; save me and I shall be saved for you are my praise." Jeremiah 17:14.

Much peace and much joy comes from a relationship with you.

The fear of the Lord is the beginning of wisdom. Righteousness exalts a nation.

Magnify the Lord with me and let us exalt his name together.

Multiplied by tens of thousands. Occupy until I come.

Make haste to do my will. All is well.

"Much grace to you, and peace be multiplied to you." 2 Peter 1:2. Love with a grateful heart.

All that I have is yours. Blessed are the righteous.

Thank you for making the "crooked places straight and the rough places smooth." Luke 3:5.

All power and might belong to you.

"Bless the Lord, o my soul, and all that is within me bless his holy name." Psalms 103:1.

Much to do.

Road to success.

"Therefore if the Son makes you free, you shall be free indeed." John 8:36.

"There is therefore now no condemnation to those who are in Christ Jesus, who walk not after the flesh but according to the Spirit." Romans 8:1.

Soon-coming King. Master of everything.

My heart's desire.

# DECEMBER 12

High upon your holy hill I come.

Thank you that you never leave me or forsake me. You are always with me. I am never alone.

"If God be for me, who can be against me?" Romans 8:31. My house is built upon the Rock, the wisdom and knowledge of Jesus Christ.

Much to do, many souls to win.

Occupy until I come. "Many are the afflictions of the righteous, but you deliver them out of them all." Psalms 34:19.

High upon your lofty hill is abundance of peace. Like rivers in the desert, you fill my thirsty soul.

"Abide in me and I will abide in you." John 15:4. Master of everything.

"I will lift up my eyes to the hills from whence comes my help? My help comes from the Lord, who made heaven and earth." Psalms 121:1.

Righteous acts of the saints. Come, Holy Spirit; my love abounds.

"Thy will be done, on earth as it is in heaven." Matthew 6:10. Speak through me, Lord. Minister through me and make me a blessing. Help me to point people to you.

"When the Enemy comes in like a flood, the Spirit of the Lord will lift up a standard against him." Isaiah 59:19.

"And no weapon formed against me will ever prosper." Isaiah 54:17. Glory to God.

They come from the north, south, east, and west.

"From the rising of the sun to its going down the Lords name is to be praised." Psalms 113:3.

My wonderful Counselor, my Prince of Peace, my all-sufficient one, my healer, my deliverer, my forgiver, my all-consuming fire, mighty God.

I seek you with all that is within me. "I am the way, the truth, and the life. No one comes to the Father except through me." John 14:6.

Cast all your care upon me, for I care for you. ("Casting all your care upon him, for he cares for you.") My ever-present help in time of need. 1 Peter 5:7.

"Mercy triumphs over judgment." James 2:13. Light of the World; lead me in the way of everlasting.

Righteous Judge, my life is in your hands.

Abundance of peace and prosperity. Much love and care.

Let bygones be bygones.

# December 14

"The Spirit of the Lord is upon me, because He has anointed me to preach the gospel to the poor; he has sent me to heal the brokenhearted, to proclaim liberty to the captives and recovery of sight to the blind, to set at liberty those who are oppressed; to proclaim the acceptable year of the Lord." Luke 4:18. The blessing of the Lord is upon me. "O magnify the Lord with me and let us exalt His name together." Psalms 34:3. Praise His holy name. Carry on.

Righteous acts of the saints. Much to do.

Abundance of peace. You will see the miracle of my grace. Peace be with you. Walk in the favor of God and the fear of the Lord. "Cast all your care upon me, for I care for you." 1 Peter 56:7. "And do not be not conformed to this world but be ye transformed by the renewing of your mind, that you may prove what is that good and acceptable and perfect will of God." Romans 12:2.

May my word transform you, righteous one.

"As each one has received a gift, minister it to one another, as good stewards of the manifold grace of God." 1 Peter 4:10. To love and be loved.

Destined to reign with abundance and peace and prosperity and wisdom from above.

Enjoy my presence and my love. Fulfill your destiny.

"My tongue is the pen of the ready writer." Psalms 45:1.

Above all else, seek me with all of your heart.

*Linda Walker*

# December 17

You are my everything. You make bitter experiences sweet. I look to you, Lord. You are my very present help in time of need. I keep my eyes focused upon you and not the circumstances around me.

Because your Word is what is truth, and I put my trust in you. "God you make a way where there seems no way." {Don Moen}. Much to do. Focus on me.

"When the Enemy comes in like a flood, the Spirit of the Lord will lift up a standard against him." Isaiah 59:19.

"Hope thou in me." Psalms 42:11. Minister of the gospel.

Surround us with songs of deliverance and guide us continually by your Holy Spirit.

Love overflowing and full of your morning glory. You own all the cattle upon the hill.

Much abundance and peace and prosperity shall be yours. Overflowing and full of your goodness.

"Rock of ages, cleft for me, let me hide myself in thee." {Augustus Montague Toplady}.

"Come to me, all you who labor and are heavy laden, and I will give you rest." Matthew 11:28.

"Let not your hearts be troubled; neither let them be afraid." John 14:27. "Seek peace and pursue it." Psalms 34:14.

Come, Holy Spirit; fill our lives with your love.

I know the plans and purposes for your life. "Come now, and let us reason together." Isaiah 1:18.

Fulfill your destiny. City on a hill. "Let your light so shine before men that they may see your good works and glorify your Father in heaven." Matthew 5:16. From this time forth and forevermore.

Richness of the Lord. Bright and shining star you are.

"Righteousness exalts a nation." Proverbs 14:34. "One nation, under God, with liberty and justice for all."

Thank you, Father, for promising us only the best, only the very best.

"Peace I leave with you, my peace I give to you; not as the world gives do I give to you. Let not your heart be troubled, neither let it be afraid." John 14:27.

Holy Ghost revival. Come, let us gather together in the bond of unity.

United we stand, divided we fall. "Seek peace and pursue it." Psalms 34:14.

Stay close to me.

Winds of revival, sweep through this land. Onward, Christian soldier.

Much to do, many to save, accomplish much. McIntosh.

Live to give. Blessed to be a blessing.

"Hope thou in me." Psalms 42:11.

# DECEMBER 20

My help comes from you, Lord. "Hope thou in me." Psalms 42:11.

Master of the universe. The rapture of the church.

"Thy kingdom come, thy will be done, on earth as it is in heaven." Matthew 6:10.

Nothing lacking and nothing missing.

"Beloved, I pray that you may prosper in all things and be in health just as your soul prospers." 3 John:2.

High upon your holy hill I come.

"Go therefore and make disciples of all the nations, baptizing them in the name of the Father, the Son, and the Holy Spirit." Matthew 28:19. Justice and mercy for all.

One God, one Lord, one Savior. Forever changed by your love. A sinner saved by grace.

Grace be upon you.

"No weapon formed against you shall prosper, and every tongue that rises against you in judgment you shall condemn." Isaiah 54:17.

Wisdom, righteousness, sanctification, and redemption belong to me, and I praise you for it!

Come, Holy Spirit. Sweep through this land. Heal hearts today. Draw people closer to you. Comfort them. Fill our hearts with joy and peace, and may sorrow and sighing flee away.

"In your presence is fullness of joy; at your right hand are pleasures forevermore." Psalms 16:11. Fill our hearts with songs of deliverance and life evermore.

"In the world you will have tribulation; but be of good cheer, I have overcome the world." John 16:33.

"Let not your hearts be troubled; neither let them be afraid." John 14:27.

"Vengeance is mine. I will repay, says the Lord." Romans 12:19.

The great Shepherd will lead and protect you. "He leads you beside the still waters; he will restore your soul. He will never leave you or forsake you. Surely goodness and mercy shall follow you all the days of your life and you will dwell in the house of the Lord forever." Psalms 23:2-6.

Righteousness overcomes evil. "Do not be overcome by evil, but overcome evil with good." Romans 12:21. "And by his stripes we are healed." 1 Peter 2:24.

"Mercy triumphs over judgment." James 2:13. Come, Holy Spirit, and heal this land.

My help comes from you, Lord, bright and morning star.

Shine into the hearts of your people and fill them with your love, joy, and peace forevermore.

Soon-coming King.

Much to do, places to go.

# DECEMBER 25

"Blessed assurance, Jesus is mine. O what a foretaste of glory divine." {Fanny J. Crosby}.

Thank you for the rain today, Lord. Thank you for your most precious gift to this world—your Son, Jesus Christ. Thank you that he was born to suffer and die, to take our sins upon his body, and all of our sicknesses and diseases, so that we would be made completely whole.

"Bless the Lord, o my soul; and all that is within me bless his holy name.

Bless the Lord, o my soul, and forget not all of his benefits; who forgives all our iniquities and who heals all of our diseases, who redeems your life from destruction, who crowns us with loving kindness and tender mercies, who satisfies our mouths with good things, so that our youth is renewed like the eagles. Bless the Lord, o my soul, and all that is within me bless His holy name." Psalms 103:1-5.

Peace, peace be upon you and within your borders.

Much joy, much happiness, much love, much forgiveness, and much fulfillment.

"Taste and see that I am good, Psalms 34:8 "and no weapon formed against me shall ever prosper." Isaiah 54:17.

Tarry with me for a while.

"Do not cast me away from your presence, and do not take thy Holy Spirit from me Father. Restore unto me the joy of my salvation and uphold me by your generous Spirit." Psalms 51:11.

You're altogether lovely. Love finds a home.

Much abundance and much peace belong to you.

The ways of the Master.

"Peace I leave with you, my peace I give to you; not as the world gives do I give to you. Let not your heart be troubled; neither let it be afraid." John 14:27.

"And the peace of God, which surpasses all understanding, will guard your hearts and minds through Christ Jesus." Philippians 4:7.

"But above all these things put on love, which is the bond of perfection." Colossians 3:14.

"O magnify the Lord with me and let us exalt His name together." Psalms 34:3.

"Forever O Lord, Your word is settled in heaven." Psalms 119:89.

Whatsoever I bind on earth is bound in heaven, and whatsoever I loose on earth is loosed in heaven. ("Assuredly, I say to you, whatever you bind on earth will be bound in heaven, and whatever you loose on earth will be loosed in heaven.")Matthew 18:18.

A call to peace. River of life flow through me.

Prosperity fills our palaces.

Marching orders.

Peace be upon you in the comfort of your own home.

Much to do.

# DECEMBER 27

"O taste and see that the Lord is good blessed is the man who trusts in Him." O come let us praise His name together. Psalms 34:8.

"Blessed are the righteous who delights greatly in his commandments. His seed shall be mighty upon this earth." Psalms 112:1-2.

Thank you, Lord, that your word is health to all of my flesh. Your word is life and health to me. ("My son, give attention to my words; incline your ear to my sayings. Do not let them depart from your eyes; keep them in the midst of your heart; for they are life to those who find them, and health to all their flesh.") Proverbs 4:20-23.

Much happiness and much peace belong to me. "Righteousness exalts a nation." Proverbs 14:34.

*Linda Walker*

Praise beautifies you. "Peace be within your walls, Prosperity within your palaces." Psalms 122:7.

Peace, peace be upon you. Righteous judge.

"Hope thou in me." Psalms 42:11. Right standing with God.

"Blessed assurance, Jesus is mine. O what a foretaste of glory divine." {Fanny J. Crosby}.

Drink in of my presence today.

The government shall be upon your shoulders and "the just shall live by faith." ("For unto us a child is born, unto us a Son is given; and the government will be upon His shoulder.") Isaiah 9:6.

Occupy until I come.

Make my way straight. Soon-coming King.

("He said, I am the voice of one crying in the wilderness; make straight the way of the Lord.") John 1:23.

"You are the light of the world. A city that is set on a hill cannot be hidden." Matthew 5:14.

Master, Savior, Prince of Peace, shine your light for all to see. Magnificent King, Majesty.

Widespread famine.

Above all else, seek me.

I am your very present help in time of trouble. ("God is our refuge and strength, a very present help in trouble.") Psalms 46:1.

Double prosperity and double abundance.

The way of the Master.

"Peace be within your walls prosperity within your palaces." Psalms 122:7.

Daily walk with thee, King of majesty.

"Hope thou in me," my righteous one. Psalms 42:11.

"Bright and morning star." Revelation 22:16

# December 28

Thank you for waking me this morning and speaking to me words of comfort and encouragement and words of faith and trust. Thank you for reminding me that you are in complete control of everything and are my provider. ("And my God shall supply all your need according to his riches in glory by Christ Jesus.") Philippians 4:19. Every need is supplied according to your riches, in glory by Christ Jesus.

You spoke "worship center" to me.

"Hope thou in me." Psalms 42:11.

"And we know that all things work together for good to those who love God, to those who are the called according to his purpose.") Romans 8:28.

"O magnify the Lord with me and let us exalt his name together." Psalms 34:3. Worship the King.

His abundant grace, grace, grace to you.

"But now, O Lord, you are our Father; we are the clay, and you our potter; and all we are the work of your hand." Isaiah 64:8. You are my potter and I am the clay.

Much wealth, much health, much prosperity, much abundance, much love, much mercy and much grace. Abundant provision and every need met.

"Not by might nor by power, but by my Spirit, saith the Lord." Zechariah 4:6.

Magnificent Savior, King of Kings, and Lord of Lord.

Much joy overflowing and full of your mercy and grace.

"O magnify the Lord with me and let us exalt His name together." Psalms 34:3. "Thy Kingdom come, thy will be done, on earth as it is in heaven." Matthew 6:10. "Righteousness exalts a nation." Proverbs 14:34.

"Grace and peace be multiplied to you in the knowledge of God and of Jesus or Lord." 2 Peter 1:2. "From the rising of the sun to the going down the Lord's name is to be praised." Psalms 113:3. Great is the Lord and greatly to be praised. Bless His Holy name.

"Unless the Lord builds the house, they labor in vain who build it." Psalms 127:1. "Count it all joy when you fall into various trials." James 1:2.

"Blessed are the peacemakers, for they shall be called the sons of God." Matthew 5:9.

"When He ascended on high, He led captivity captive, and gave gifts to men." Ephesians 4:8.

"Do not touch my anointed ones, and do my prophets no harm." Psalms 105:15.

Peace be upon you, go in peace.

# December 30

"From the rising of the sun to its going down the Lord's name is to be praised." Psalms 113:3. Praise ye the Lord.

March madness.

My soul waits for thee. Wonder of wonders.

"O magnify the Lord with me and let us exalt his name together." Psalms 34:3. Praise beautifies.

Come and let us worship the King.

Praise ye the Lord.

You are abundantly blessed. Peace be upon you. My glory shall be seen upon you and I will give you rest.

"Thy kingdom come, thy will be done, on earth as it is in heaven." Matthew 6:10.

Mercy Ministries.

You set the solidarity in families. ("God sets the solitary in families; he brings out those who are bound into prosperity.") Psalms 68:6.

Much abundance and overflowing joy belongs to you. Much peace and righteousness and the favor of the Lord will chase you and overtake you and the fear of the Lord.

Your love overshadows me.

Healing is thy portion.

*Linda Walker*

# December 31

"Grace and peace by multiplied to you." 2 Peter 1:2. As I meditate upon your Word, peace and joy fill my heart.

The way of the Master. His ways are not my ways, and his thoughts are not my thoughts.

As I meditate upon your Word, day and night I shall make my way prosperous and I shall have good success. World-overcoming faith. ("This book of the law shall not depart from your mouth, but you shall meditate in it day and night, that you may observe to do according to all that is written in it. For then you will make your way prosperous, and then you will have good success.") Joshua 1:8.

"Now thanks be to God who always leads us in triumph in Christ, and through us diffuses the fragrance of his knowledge in every place." 2 Corinthians 2:14.

Redundant.

Peace, peace I leave with you. "Cast your bread upon the waters, for you will find it after many days." Ecclesiastes 11:1.

"Whispering Pines."

Stretch forth your hand to the needy.

"Thy kingdom come, thy will be done, on earth as it is in heaven." Matthew 6:10.

"Be still and know that I am God." Psalms 46:10.

**In Jesus' name. Amen.**